Christians Under Construction

by
Dr. Staccato Powell and
Dr. Dennis Proctor

Christians Under Construction

by

Dr. Staccato Powell and

Dr. Dennis Proctor

KAIROS PRESS

Baltimore, Maryland

Unless otherwise indicated, all Scripture quotations are taken from the *King James Version of the Bible*. Some quotations are from the *New International Version*.

Christians Under Construction
ISBN 0-9646729-0-1
Copyright © 1996 by
Staccato Powell
613 N. Garrison Ave., St. Louis, MO 63103
Dennis Proctor
1128 Pennsylvania Ave., Baltimore, MD 21201

Published by Kairos Press
P.O. Box 21237
Baltimore, MD 21228
410-728-7416

Acknowledgments

In the words of a mutual mentor, no man is a giant, but a mere pygmy standing on another's shoulder. This is definitely an accurate description of each one of us. For if we have any stature at all, it is due to the elevation provided by the many pillars upon which we stand.

We pause to pay homage to those who illumined the prodigious path on which we plod. The Episcopal Fathers of our beloved African Methodist Episcopal Zion Church, both active and retired, mortal and immortal, have impacted our lives in no small measure.

Laboring together as pastors on the banks of the Cape Fear River in North Carolina, we were influenced by the tutelage of the Right Reverend Reuben Lee Speaks. Senior Bishop Speaks constantly compelled us to strive for excellence spiritually, morally, and intellectually. His firm compassionate admonition to pray hard, work hard, and live right has consistently challenged us.

Due to the godly judgment and appointive authority of the Right Reverends Milton A. Williams and Enoch B. Rochester, we serve in our present pastoral capacities. We are eternally grateful to these two episcopates for perusing the landscape of pulpiteers and picking two of the least to serve as undershepherds of two of Zion's great congregations. Two members of the 1992 Episcopal class, the Right

Reverends Marshall H. Strickland and Clarence Carr, left to each of us a legacy of leadership. We now stand at the helm of vessels these two clerics navigated through capricious channels.

Words are inadequate to express our debt of gratitude to the Right Reverends Cecil Bishop, George Walker, Samuel C. Ekemam, Sr., George Battle, Joseph Johnson, and Richard Thompson for the varied and sundry opportunities provided us to share our gifts of service in their episcopal vineyards. Whether we had the opportunity to preach, teach, pray, or simply be present in their area, we were blessed as a result.

Our colleagues and co-laborers are too numerous to mention by name. Each of you know who you are and what your camaraderie and companionship has meant to us. We thank you for friendship and fellowship.

When we embarked upon this literary task we could not fathom how stratospheric our ambitions were. These ambitions would have remained earth-bound without the painstaking prayers and tedious transcription of Lottie B. Lewis.

Although we undertook the effort of writing, we do not profess to be grammarians. We turned to a friend in the personage of Mrs. Mary Frances Lane Delaney who did a marvelous job in proofing the original manuscript.

This publishing feat has been accomplished in large measure because of the technical assistance of James A. Ferrier. Jim's professionalism, patience, and prodding provided the grist for the mill to make this project possible. His efficient and expeditious work ethic was par excellence.

Just when we felt we had sufficiently prepared the manuscript for publication, the sagacious scholar, Dr. Samuel Dewitt Proctor, advised "not yet!" Though the release of this work was delayed, we will be forever grateful to this peerless progenitor of pulpit scholastics and ambassador of African-American academicians for his wise counsel. Dr. Proctor, thanks for sparing us from scouring the country in years to come, asking the unenviable question, "Have you seen our book?"

Most significant mention must be of those who know us best — those who love us unconditionally. Our families who share intimate moments of inspiration are the true heroes. The wives of our youth, Diane Proctor and Susan Powell, respectively, who pray with and for us, were indispensable in this process. The children, Emory, Dennis, and Diandra Proctor, and Staccato and Susan Powell are their fathers' darlings and delights. Thanks, guys, for keeping us humble. We have immeasurable affection and appreciation for each of you.

The congregations we serve, Pennsylvania Avenue and Washington Metropolitan, have in many ways provided the necessary crucible for our faith formation. Each congregation has contributed significantly to our prayer life.

We have come a long way. Therefore, we are indebted to a great cloud of witnesses. Space is inadequate and mental faculties incapable for any attempt at naming all who have assisted in one way or another. Suffice it to say we appreciate every act of support.

We sincerely hope and pray our effort will have a transformational impact on those who dare to delve in the direction of the Divine.

Contents

Dedication

To our fallen fathers whose faith, fortitude, and friendship bridge the chasm that exists from earth to glory.

For the lessons they taught, one with the plow and the other with the pulpit, we rise and call them blessed:

The Rev. Emory Clement Proctor:
1907-1989
Mr. Harry Sylvester Powell, Sr.:
1924-1994

Introduction

As we minister to many, we are made acutely aware of the constant struggle and striving toward the mark for the prize of the high calling of God in Christ Jesus. (Phil. 3:14.)

Our constant prayer is, "Lord, I want to be a Christian in my heart."

One of life's realities, however, is that we are not what we are going to be. By God's grace and with our willingness, there is much more joy to come in every Christian's life. Jesus' promise and purpose is *life more abundantly*.

Life is dynamic, not static. For any of us to refer to ourselves as being *Christian* is, in a real sense, a misnomer. What we all discover, as life progresses after our conversions, is that it is more appropriate to describe oneself as *becoming a Christian*.

Becoming a real Christian requires a commitment to personal spirituality. One must be willing to espouse the necessary work ethic to engage in the ongoing process of allowing God to build, or construct, "carnal" self into a Christian man or woman. This endeavor requires a major investment of time, energy, effort, and dedication.

As two "becoming-Christians" who are employed and engaged as both "general and sub-contractors" (pastors), we are personally cognizant of the necessity to persistently and prayerfully construct Christians. We hasten to add that we are not ourselves exempt (pastors), we are personally cognizant of the necessity to persistently and prayerfully construct Christians. We hasten to add that we are not ourselves exempt from the construction process. We also are personal projects being built by the Master Craftsman: God. In many instances, we plead patience "for God is not through with us yet"!

The Apostle Paul understood the fact of construction very clearly, writing late in his ministry that he himself was not complete.

> **Not as though I had already attained, either were already perfect: but I follow after, if that I may apprehend that for which also I am apprehended of Christ Jesus.**
>
> **Philippians 3:12**

We recognize the ongoing struggle involved in the building process. Every day finds each of us utilizing the requisite tools and instruments of the "trade." There are specific materials that must go into the building of Christians. These materials also must be of a certain quality.

Each "building" (Christian) must be constructed according to the specifications and designs drawn by the Architect. In order for a certificate of occupation to be issued by a housing or building inspector, there must be conformity to the appropriate codes. Those codes for Christians are established by the One Who serves as Architect, Craftsman, and Inspector.

We sincerely trust, hope, and pray that what we share in these pages will assist you in "passing inspection." We request that our readers' prayers include the favorable mentioning of our names in order that, as we attempt to minister to others, we ourselves not be lost.

> **But I keep under my body, and bring it into subjection: lest that by any means, when I have preached to others, I myself should be a castaway.**
>
> **1 Corinthians 9:27**

The ultimate aim of the Church is to have the Inspector certify each Christian as a "good and faithful servant." (Matt. 25:21,23.)

1
Christians Under Construction

What is a Christian?

Is it one who professes a belief in the person and the teachings of Jesus Christ?

Is it one who may not believe in, but practices, the tenets of the Christ message?

Is a Christian one who belongs to a certain church or communion?

Does the spouse-beating, profane-speaking, vow-breaking, baptized, choir member have more standing with God than the philanthropic, self-sacrificing, commitment-cherishing atheist?

Is there an initiation or pledge period required for attainment of the name "Christian"?

Is "Christian" a vicarious or intergenerational bequeathment awarded to families for faithful service?

The story is told of a man who stood proudly to address a Sunday School assembly. He wore a smartly tailored suit, expensive jewelry, and spoke with an air of distinction.

"Children, I was a founding member of this church, I am the largest contributor, and

15

I haven't missed a Sunday in twenty-six years. Why do you think they call me a Christian?" he asked presumptuously.

His wife, sitting in the rear of the auditorium, responded under her breath, "Because they don't know you!"

———————

Could the inherent ambiguity in interpretation of the word Christian (*Christianos* in the Greek) be the reason for its appearance only three times in the New Testament?

For the purposes of our text, we define a *Christian* as "one professing faith in the person of Jesus Christ, the Son of the living God, with a desire to live in accordance with His teachings and precepts as recorded in the Bible." Ours is an orthodox view of Jesus Christ promulgated at the Council of Chalcedon, A.D. 451, which holds "that in one person, Jesus Christ, there are two natures, a human and a divine, each with completeness and integrity."[1]

The term *construction* denotes the "building or erecting of an entity, idea or conversation." Hence, a *Christian under construction* is "one who has made a profession of faith and is at once in pursuit of possession of the same." Modern parlance would describe a Christian as someone not only willing to "talk the talk, but walk the walk" of a Christ-like one.[2]

Is a Christian under construction an oxymoronic phase, one that is self-contradicting?

How can one who is a believer and follower of Jesus Christ be in need of structural and spiritual maintenance?

Do the doctrines of justification, adoption, and sanctification not negate the need for continued post confessional modification?

Does the efficacy of Christ's ignominious death not cover our character, conduct, and credibility now, henceforth, and forever more?

A cursory glance at the aforementioned doctrines speak to what God does for the believer. The construction of which we speak encapsulates what God does in and with the believer.

Justification is simply defined as:

> . . . A judicial act of God by which, on account of Christ, to whom the sinner is united by faith, He declares that sinner to be no longer exposed to the penalty of the law, but to be restored to His favor . . . . Justification is the reversal of God's attitude toward the sinner because of the sinner's new relation to Christ.[3]

Justification does not make one righteous, but declares one righteous. This distinction allows for a chasm to exist between creed and deed. It affords one an opportunity to put on the uniform of the Holy, while denying the power and practice thereof.

Having received the imputation of divine righteousness, the convert (Christian) is eligible for, and receives, adoption into the divine family. This concept, though avoided by some theologians, provides a helpful and pragmatic understanding of this lesser-known doctrine of the Christian faith.

Adoption is a legally significant binding relationship. It provides family name, inheritance, and standing. It however does not ensure family resemblance, attributes, or affection. An individual can be adopted into a family of virtue, values, and veracity, yet the same individual may bring shame, disapproval, and heartache to those who bestowed unrequired allegiance to him.

Sanctification, like justification and adoption in its true essence bespeaks an activity of God toward the believer. By such, God "sets the believer apart" for the purposes of the kingdom.

In the Old Testament, men, beasts, mountains, seasons, buildings were candidates for sanctification.

The New Testament concept relates to the ceremonial separation, thus putting one in position to be utilized in service of the Lord. (2 Tim. 2:21.)

It is most unfortunate that the same vessels who are sanctified or set apart for heavenly use can be unwitting emissaries of hell. Tragic indeed are the ordained of God who have abandoned their first love, or who from time to time have forgotten to whom they are espoused. Doctrines do not a Christian make.

What God does for us is rarely reflected in what we do for God. What should the response of a soul saved and secured by Christ be?

The Apostle Paul, grappling with the response and responsibility to the high calling of the Christ, provided a paradigm or outline for us to show the way to a more perfect pilgrimage. Paul wrote his epistle of encouragement and commendation to the Philippians from the confinement of a prison cell, speaking of the construction he was currently experiencing.

Not as though I had already obtained, wither were already perfect: but I follow after, if that I may apprehend that for which also I am apprehended of Christ Jesus.

Brethren, I count not myself to have apprehended: but this one thing I do, forgetting those things which are behind, and reaching forth unto those things which are before.

I press toward the mark for the prize of the high calling of God in Christ Jesus.

Philippians 3:12-14

One may be surprised to find Paul taking the time to write such a reflective and reviving message while sitting in a prison cell. Scholars differ as to which imprisonment was responsible for this letter. Whether imprisoned in Caesarea, Ephesus, or Rome, Paul demonstrated that shackles on the body need not enfeeble and incarcerate the soul. Indeed, on a previous occasion (Acts 16), Paul discovered that a facility used for an unfair beating could be transformed by the power of faith into a temple of praise and a ground-shaking prayer meeting.

Can anyone of contemporary analysis fail to appreciate the immeasurable contribution the pen of prison produced in John Milton's *Paradise Lost*, or John Bunyan's *Pilgrim's Progress*, or the logography developed by Victor Frankl via the concentration camps of Auschwitz and Dachau, or the magna carta of a movement embodied in Martin Luther King, Jr.'s "Letter from a Birmingham Jail." At present, your lot in life may not be what you desire or deserve, but remember that God's presence can transcend the trauma of the moment and transform tragedy into triumph.

Not only does Paul display an immunity to adversity, but he demonstrates a fidelity to friendship. His current hardship was not sufficient to erase the memory of generosity displayed by the Philippian church. How refreshing it is to notice a person of meager means expressing gratitude for life's little blessings. An anonymous poet captured the essence of this spirit when he wrote,

Today upon a bus I saw
A lovely maid with golden hair;
I envied her — she seemed so gay
And oh, I wished I were so fair,
When suddenly she rose to leave,
I saw her hobble down the aisle;
She had one foot and wore a crutch,
But as she passed, she had a smile.
Oh God, forgive me when I whine:
I have two feet — the world is mine.

The poet continues to examine the joy of sight and hearing and concludes by saying:

With feet to take me where I'd go,
With eyes to see the sunset's glow,
With ears to hear what I would know;
I'm blessed indeed. The world is mine;
Oh God, forgive me when I whine!

It is evident that Paul's nurturing of the relationship with the Christians at Philippi when he was strong afforded him the luxury of relying on and relating to them at the time of his infirmity. The truth of the proverbial saying rings with crystal clarity, "Be kind to the people you meet on your way up, for you may see the same faces on your way back down."

Paul was aware that there were some in the church who were blinded by love, devotion or just hierarchical allegiance, and wanted to exalt him to the pedestal of perfection. To which Paul said in essence, "With humility I accept your assessment, however, I have not yet apprehended. . . ." This statement divides neatly into a homiletical outline. There are three dimensions of sight that Paul experienced as a result of his self-examination or catharsis of the soul. These same stages are necessary for the construction of every Christian.

Three States of Construction

Insight

The first stage is found in Paul's statement, "I do not consider myself yet to have taken hold. . . ." That showed insight into his own character and development as a Christ-follower.

We often are tempted to live in self-congratulatory arenas of acceptance. We live in a society where disclosure is rare and self-disclosure is nearly non-existent. This deception is rarely the result of malice aforethought, but a response to a "teflon age" that encourages one to "fake it until you make it." Self-examination is difficult; self-correction is more difficult. But the latter depends upon the former. Therapists speak of this in terms of denial — the protecting of self from unpleasant reality by refusal to perceive or face it.[4] Although at times helpful as an ego-defense mechanism, denial more often than not leads to fantasy, repression, rationalization, emotional isolation, and scores of other maladaptive social responses. There is a children's story entitled, "The Emperor's New Clothes," in which an emperor failed to accept that he was clad only in his underwear until a child spoke up and ended his delusion.

For the Christian, sin has the same anaesthetizing effect. After all, "nobody's perfect," "everybody has some vice," "at least I'm not guilty of . . . ," and the list goes on *ad infinitum*. However, the issue is not how one stacks up to self-imposed standards or people-imposed standards, but how does one fare in the *sub spacia teletochtaes* under the gaze of God.

Paul understood that under the Mosaic law he was blameless, a "pharisee of the pharisees." But under the rubric of a follower of Christ, he had been "weighed in the balance and found wanting." Paul was in essence confessing his error. In the Greek, confession is defined *homologeo*, "the ability to see one's actions as God sees them." *Insight* causes Christians to admit, acknowledge, and agree that they have missed the mark. Insight causes one to personally apply the adage that "the largest room in the world is − room for improvement."

It is no wonder that in the seventh chapter of Romans, Paul would assert "when I would do good evil is present with me." The insightful Christian can assert with humility of spirit, "I am not what I ought to be!"

Thank goodness Paul did not stop there on what Howard Thurman would call his inward journey.[5] He continues the discourse, expressing the second stage: "Forgetting what is behind."

Hindsight

The journey now moves to its second dimension. Paul does not suffer here from regressive delusional

22

projection, or "I wish I would have, should have, could have."

Instead, he uses the 20/20 vision of hindsight to free himself from the inertia caused by a preoccupation with the faults, failures, and fears of the past. None of us can boast of a past free of poor decisions, hasty actions, procrastination, prevarications, and an endless list of better-forgotten responses to the ebb and flow of life.

A view of the past should serve as a milestone to guide us, not a millstone to grind us.

As a Christian under construction one must learn to forget the gratification that is associated with self (soul) destructive and distracting tendencies. This is often easier said than done. Science has recently made the faith community aware of the physiological cravings that often war against spiritual and psychological resolve.

Opium-like substances produced in the brain and pituitary gland called *endorphins* can be triggered by a number of stimuli.[6] Unfortunately, these endorphins remind one of a pleasurable experience while nullifying the pain. For example, hearing a favorite song that was "special" to a couple may reignite feelings of longing and cause loneliness.

The endorphins remind you of picnics and pleasant times. However, the reality is that those memories may be from "day one" of a romance that was wrought with infidelity, neglect, and sadness.

Forgetting necessitates that we view our faults as fault lines that render us vulnerable at the core of our being. Thus we may take special precautions to guard self from self. (Eph. 4:27.) This concept was mentioned long years before the Apostle Paul by the psalmist who declared in Psalm 119:67,71:

> **Before I was afflicted I went astray, but now I have kept thy Word.**
>
> **It is good for me that I have been afflicted; that I might learn thy statutes.**

Mistakes are of no value unless the lessons learned from them point to a more productive and prosperous life, and lead "not into temptation, but deliver us from evil." One must not only forget negatives associated with faults, failures, and fears, but sometimes good fortune can lull one into a sense of self-reliance and spiritual complacency. For some prosperity is more difficult to handle than adversity. The stigma of sackcloth is more enriching to the soul than the beauty of broadcloth.

Paul's disclaimer is thought by many scholars to be a renunciation of all that was not in keeping with the mind of Christ. To that end Paul was able to count all as "dung" (Phil. 3:8) except what he knew in Christ Jesus.

The Christian with a heartfelt hindsight should be able to say, "I am not what I used to be."

The journey now proceeds to its third and decisive dimension: "I press on toward the goal (mark)."

Foresight

A poet has placed in perspective life's paradisiacal pursuit in his familiar couplet:

Heaven is not gained in a single bound,
but we mount its summit round by round.

Those not as familiar with literary legends have pronounced the pilgrimage in equally poignant prose:

We are climbing Jacob's ladder,
Every round goes higher, higher.

It is in this posture that Paul provides the foresight sufficient to obtain motivation and sustain inspiration. There are those who critique this concept as being "other worldly" or eschatological, and as such devoid of relevance in the pragmatic development of the Christian.

However these words reflect an existential understanding of one's reach exceeding one's grasp. The achievements of today become the springboards for tomorrow's strivings. In essence, Paul concluded the trilogy by saying, "I'm not what I'm going to be."

The tripartite revelation of *insight, hindsight, and foresight* becomes a montage of life experiences, with the individual experiencing what Friedreich Schleiermacher referred to as the *sensus numinus*. African-American ancestors, unfamiliar with theological terminology from the academy, understood the phenomenon all too well and described it appropriately in song:

I looked at my hands and they looked new,
I looked at my feet and they were too.

These are not the mutterings of those expressing infantile prelogical ideation, but rather give evidence to what Howard Thurmond called the "invisible tools of the spirit."

25

Using a construction motif, it could be said that the Christian under construction is built with expandable walls. These Christians are equipped to receive expanded grace, mercy, peace, wholeness, temperance, and the abundance of fruitful evidences of the Spirit.

Johnson Oatman, Jr. gives encouragement and instruction for those who would engage in this Christian sojourn in the old familiar and beloved hymn, *Higher Ground*.

> I'm pressing on the upward way,
> New heights I'm gaining ev'ry day,
> Still praying as I'm onward bound,
> "Lord, plant My feet on higher ground."

Endnotes

[1] Bancroft, Emery. *Christian Theology*, (Grand Rapids: Zondervan Publishing Co., 1976), p. 98.

[2] Cherry, Diana P.

[3] Bancroft, pp. 253,254.

[4] Freud, Ann. *Abnormal Psychology*, 1949, p. 64.

[5] Thurmond, Howard. *Inward Journey*. (Richmond: Friends United Press, 1971).

[6] Freud, Glossary, p. VII.

2
Calculate the Cost

Dietrich Bonhoeffer's classic literary tour de force, *The Cost of Discipleship*,[1] contains a line which has a chilling effect upon the desire to become definitively Christian by following Jesus the Christ. According to Bonhoeffer, when Christ calls a man, He bids him to come and die. This caveat is hardly the kind of encouragement which would convince anyone considering a decision to construct a Christian life to do so.

Although not particularly encouraging, Bonhoeffer's comment on what an affirmative response to embark on this Christian journey entails is painfully enlightening and insightful. When we consider the words "come and die," it compels us to "begin with the end in mind."

The terms of discipleship are declared plainly by great leaders. King Arthur bound his knights "by so strait vows to his own self" that they were dazed as if "half-blinded at the coming of a light."[2] Those who followed Martin Luther King, Jr. during the sixties had to renounce the use of violence even as a means of retaliation.

However, no leader asked such "strait vows," in inner and outer demand, as Jesus. We, like the multitudes of old, are diverse in our desires. Some people are revolutionary, wanting Jesus to be a firebrand. Others are impulsive, offering Him wild vows of allegiance, and of course, the self-seekers are ready to cultivate Jesus' company for personal gain. Only a few ever see in Jesus the totality of fulfillment.

Jesus is candid regarding the criteria and conditions of constructing character which mirrors the Christ. He never gilded the lily. Unlike some modern messengers, Jesus never took advantage of the psychology of success. Never did the Christ attempt to soften the blow by promising a problemless, peril-free, prosperous pilgrimage. Quite the contrary, Jesus set forth the cost and conditions of discipleship in austere terms. They were so stern, they winnowed the crowd like a fan winnowing wheat.

Nestled within the context of Jesus' journey to Jerusalem are these words:

> **If any man come to me and hate not his father, and mother, and wife, and children, and brethren, and sisters, yes, and his own life also, he cannot be my disciple.**
>
> **And whosoever doth not bear his cross, and come after me, cannot be my disciple.**
>
> **For which of you, intending to build a tower, sitteth not down first, and counteth the cost, whether he have sufficient to finish it?**
>
> **Lest haply, after he hath laid the foundation, and is not able to finish it, all that behold it begin to mock him,**
>
> **Saying, This man began to build, and was not able to finish.**
>
> **Or what king, going to make war against another king, sitteth not down first, and consulteth whether he be able with ten thousand to**

meet him that cometh against him with twenty thousand?

Or else, while the other is yet a great way off, he sendeth an ambassage, and desireth conditions of peace.

So likewise, whosoever he be of you that forsaketh not all that he hath, he cannot be my disciple.

Salt is good: but if the salt have lost his savour, wherewith shall it be seasoned?

It is neither fit for the land, nor yet for the dunghill; but men cast it out. He that hath ears to hear, let him hear.

Luke 14:26-35

This historic and epoch trek begins at Luke 9:51: **And it came to pass, when the time was come that he should be received up, he stedfastly set his face to go to Jerusalem.** Many along the way may have thought this was a "war march" at the end of which Jesus would confront leaders and cause a coup d'etat by toppling the authorities and ushering in the long-awaited and anticipated Kingdom of God. There is no surprise that the entourage following Jesus was large and enthusiastic. Many were tagging along whom He had not summoned to a life of discipleship.

Prior to this point Jesus had retreated from the public sector. Until this time, He was mainly in homes, huddling with and ministering to small enclaves. Jesus' return to the public arena was greeted by a marching multitude.

The issue facing Jesus was not reluctance but enthusiasm. Some thought it was a parade. It sounds much like a modern ticker-tape parade. The cause for the exuberation, exhilaration, and excitement was irrelevant. It was a parade, a public event that required no permission or invitation to join. Soon, however, Jesus would commence a conversation that would cut to the quick and penetrate this emotional euphoric enthusiasm.

In so doing, Jesus employed an observable didactic refrain formula: **Whosoever does not . . . cannot be my disciple**. He filled the blank with staggering, sobering, terse words demanding deep, thought-provoking decision making.

Come and Die

In calculating the cost of constructing a Christian life, there are some pragmatic considerations that should be stated initially and generally. Often those who ascribe to the Christian ethic are the objects of ridicule and insult. Friends may no longer desire your presence. Even close family members may find your fellowship disdainful.

However, the onus is placed upon the individual who contemplates going the way of Christ. Jesus makes this clear in addressing the multitude as recorded in the concluding pericope of Luke 14.

Discipleship Can Be Lonely

Bonhoeffer poignantly picks up the particularization of the nature of the call in his chapter, "Discipleship and the Individual," which he bases on this same gospel passage. According to Bonhoeffer:

> Through the call of Jesus, men become individuals. Willy-nilly, they are compelled to decide, and that decision can only be made

by themselves. It is Christ who makes them individuals by calling them. Every one is called separately and must follow alone. But people are frightened by solitude, and they try to protect themselves from it by merging themselves in the society of their fellows and in their material environment.

They become suddenly aware of their responsibilities and duties, and are loath to part with them. But all this is only a cloak to protect them from having to make a decision. They are unwilling to stand alone before Jesus and to be compelled to decide with their eyes fixed on him alone. Yet neither father nor mother, neither wife nor child, neither nationality nor tradition can protect a man at the moment of his call. It is Christ's will that he should be thus isolated, and that he should fix his eyes solely upon Him.[3]

When one starts to count the cost of construction, the words of Jesus sting and repel. To begin with, Jesus warned that whosoever does not hate family and his or her own life could not be His disciple. (Luke 14:26.)

This is a challenge to rearrange personal or individual priorities. The word *hate* means "to turn away from/to detach oneself from." Hate must not be confused or weakened to mean a mere comparative lovelessness which implies still loving a little. What is at issue here is loyalty rather than affection.

Within the contractor's calculation for the erection of an edifice, some materials are priority. So, in the network of the many loyalties in which all of us live, the claim of Christ and the demands of the Gospel must not only take precedence but must redefine the others.

Jesus is not requesting self-loathing or self-pity. Jesus is requiring that the claim of Christ and the demands of the Gospel be first and foremost as well as determine and dictate how life is lived. Christian principles must in some way be translated into human life, and it is in the sphere of the material, in state and society, that responsible love has to be manifested.[4]

This stern statement is seemingly counter to, and flies in the face of, the contemporary clamor of the modern moral right's emphasis on family values. It causes one to wonder how former Vice President Dan Quayle would respond to such a controlling command. Certainly Jesus was not minimizing the significance of family ties.

He demanded a primary and undivided allegiance. Jesus, the lover of little children, was not despising natural ties. He blessed the children, instructed us to address God as Abba, Father, and provided for His own mother at His death by commending her into the care of a beloved disciple.

Yet, He asked instant and unqualified loyalty — certainly proof positive of a divine claim!

We can see why ships that go by the shore lights would make the ocean ways a threat; the only chance of safety on the sea is that all ships shall take their bearings from the sky.[5]

Unless our human loyalties are unified and purified by a supreme devotion, they clash and become debased. There was a day when Jesus Himself practiced what He demanded, He had to choose between home and God: Who is my mother, or my brethren? (Mark 3:33-35.)

For whosoever shall do the will of God, the same is my brother, and my sister, and mother (v. 35).

It is one thing to hate family, but even more one's own life. This is antithetical to a prevailing narcissism that pervades present day market-driven society. That strange word hate is the one road to abiding love. Our prayer concerning love of self must become that of eighteenth-century Bishop Joseph Butler:

Help us, by the due exercise of them, to improve to Perfection: till all partial Affection be lost in that entire universal one, and Thou, O God, shalt be all in all.[6]

Discipleship Rearranges Priorities

Discipleship demands that you rearrange your priorities. Bonhoeffer also wrote:

The life of discipleship can only be maintained so long as nothing is allowed to come between Christ and ourselves — neither the law, nor personal piety, nor even the world.[7]

Cost calculation compels us to re-orientate our personal pleasures. We do not have to relinquish personal pleasures, but it is imperative to reorientate the pleasure principle. This can be done when we come to terms with the great truth that *life is difficult*. According to author M. Scott Peck, once we truly see this truth, we transcend it. Life's difficulties can be solved with discipline.

> Without discipline one can solve nothing.
>
> With only some discipline we can solve only some problems.
>
> With total discipline we can solve all problems.[8]

What we are suggesting is what Peck terms "delayed gratification":

> Delaying gratification is a process of scheduling the pain and pleasure of life in such a way as to enhance the pleasure of meeting and experiencing the pain first and getting it over with. It is the only decent way to live.[9]

Jesus admonished that whosoever does not carry his or her own cross and come after him could not be His disciple. Contrary to popular understanding, one's "cross" does not mean the calamity, illness or tragedy with which we may have to live. A "cross" is doing deliberately that which you are under no obligation or compulsion to do. The mention of the cross should have struck at the heart of the crowd's enthusiasm which Jesus wanted to penetrate, but they were too excited to take notice.

In following Jesus, there is a consciousness that requires sober decision making and a calculation of the cost involved. Following Jesus is not a mindless decision one makes. To perform that which you are under no compulsion to do does not mean no thinking, testing of the will, or decision making takes place. All of those do need to happen. All are required. Decision-making is an intricate part of cost counting.

Charles W. Everest in poetry set to music states:

Take up thy cross, the Savior said,
  if thou wouldest My disciple be;
Deny thyself, the world forsake,
  and humbly follow after Me.

Take up thy cross and follow Christ,
  nor think till death to lay it down;
For only those who bear the cross
  may hope to wear the glorious crown.[10]

In the next refrain formula, Jesus highlights the necessity for cost counting. An accurate assessment of what is required for completing construction is essential. Often in haste to see the finished product, we fail to consider the fundamentals, and that causes us to miscalculate and miss some crucial steps in the process.

Stephen Covey offers a suggestion as to how we may avoid miscalculation. He says we are "to begin with the end in mind."[11] That means to start with a clear understanding of your destination. It means to know where you are going so that you better understand where you are now to ensure that the steps you take are always in the right direction. Process is as important as the finished product.

Jesus' ministry was quite illustrative of counting the cost. He portrayed the indispensability of weighing the factors in a pair of parables. The first involved a building indicative of the age in which He lived. The builder had undertaken the task of building without first ascertaining the cost for completion, which resulted in an unfinished building. (Luke 14:28-30.)

> **For which of you, intending to build a tower, sitteth not down first, and counteth the cost, whether he have sufficient to finish it?** (v. 28.)

Purportedly it was an age of unfinished towers. Even King Herod was a careless, reckless, blundering builder. He would plan lavish palaces, only to initiate construction and later determine that he could ill afford such splendor, resulting in an unfinished product.

There are two schools of thought relating to the intent of the Master teacher for sharing this story. Some are of the opinion that Jesus told the parable to justify His own caution. He could neither risk nor afford to select persons who would not continue loyal. Another view is that Jesus commanded we calculate the cost. Inasmuch as the entire pericope concerns discipleship, this slant seems most likely. However, both interpretations have merit.

The issue here is not an appeal to the fear of failure. There is no caveat, but there is sharp warning against a merely impulsive loyalty and a jaunty discipleship. You should ask yourself:

"Can I live by the Beatitudes, which are a high tower?

"Can I endure loneliness for Christ's sake?"

Do we possess patience and vision enough to construct a cathedral or build the tower of the kingdom in this tumultuous world?

Two Reasons To Count the Cost

Jesus offered two specific reasons why a person should calculate the cost: 1) a person's failure to finish may lead to frustration, causing one to erroneously conclude, "I am a failure," and 2) such failure would provoke the ridicule of the godless, thus bringing the kingdom into disrepute.

For these reasons a person has no right to play flirtatiously and loosely with the claims of Christ. A person has no right to begin the Christian life in crude and crass self-confidence. One can hurt self and the cause of Christ by carelessly committing to the campaign. Yet, one should still consider treading the trek after first calculating the cost.

Stress is placed on the conditions of discipleship through the second parable. Jesus advises us to measure the strength of the foe before joining the crusade. He asked in a rhetorical sense about a king contemplating waging war against another king counting his troops and considering the odds for victory. (Luke 14:31,32.)

Two possible explanations are offered for this counsel. Some theorize that Jesus was saying He must compute the power of the adversary and be certain of His comrades' commitment. He knew a meaningful contest cannot be conducted with frail, feeble soldiers. The second view is that our Captain may well have been cautioning us to size up the enemy, so as to avert crushing defeat through underestimation of the foe. Both views have validity.

There is little doubt that impulsive followers were the intended audience of the story. Essentially there is no difference in the two referenced parables, but perhaps there is a mood difference. The tower may be a tower of defense, the war is clearly a crusade. What a candid admission of desperate odds! The odds are two to one! What is Jesus telling us?

Could Jesus be saying to us that those who choose to follow Him are in the minority, a tattered battalion?

This is a "reality check." Prospective Christians are not informed: "You propose a warfare, not against flesh and blood, but against powers and principalities. Do you think you can prevail? If not, better not begin and invite certain defeat to the cause of Christ!" However, this is the reality!

Jesus dealt with people who desired to follow Him in this regard. He wanted to make certain their readiness involved regard for the power of the foe. We need to be mindful that our foes lie ambushed within, as well as like stalking lions without.

In both of the parables, Jesus used in the latter portion of Luke 14, the builder and the king were faced with the demand to make a determination. They were confronted with a major expenditure of time and property and life itself:

Does this cost more than you are willing to pay?

Every would-be disciple of Jesus has the same decision to make when invited or challenged with the call to construct a Christian character. Enthusiasm for beginning may be present, but you must ask yourself, "Do I possess the resources to carry through to completion?" Remember the Ecclesiastical proverb:

> ... **The race is not to the swift, nor the battle to the strong, neither yet bread to the wise, nor**

yet riches to men of understanding, nor yet favour to men of skill; but time and chance happeneth to them all.

Ecclesiastes 9:11

Jesus admonished the crowd that those called to a life of discipleship must be prepared for a loyalty which would sacrifice the dearest things in life. He warned of a suffering which would be like the agony of a person upon a cross. Jesus went on to show that, just as salt can lose its taste, so can initial commitment and enthusiasm, however sincere, fade in the course of time. (Matt. 5:13.)

Once "Jerusalem" (in the context of Jesus' journey, Jerusalem is symbolic of a spiritual place of suffering and death) becomes a very present and painful reality, commitment will be severely tested and enthusiasm will quickly wane. Under pressure, even from family, both open and subtle, "salt" does not decide to become pepper. It simply loses its taste gradually and then becomes good for nothing, not even worth walking on.

Embarking upon the Christian journey calls for careful calculation. What Jesus states about the call to discipleship is similar to what is cautioned in the marriage ceremony. It is therefore not to be entered into carelessly, casually, hurriedly, or thoughtlessly, but prayerfully, soberly, freely, advisedly, and in the fear of God.

Endnotes

[1] Bonhoeffer, Dietrich. *The Cost of Discipleship*, (New Macmillan Publishing Co., 1963), p. 79.

[2] Tennyson, Alfred Lord. *The Idylls of the King*, "The Co of King Arthur." (New York: Random House, 1938), p. 444.

[3] *Cost of Discipleship*, "Discipleship and the Individual."

[4] Ibid.

[5] Fox, Selina Fitzherbert. *A Chain of Prayer Across America*, (New York: E. P. Dutton, and Co., 1943), p. 31.

[6] Butler, Bishop Joseph.

[7] Bonhoeffer, p. 192.

[8] Peck, M. Scott. *The Road Less Traveled*, (New York: Simon and Schuster, 1978), pp. 15,16.

[9] Ibid.

[10] Everest, Charles W., (Nashville: Abingdon Press, 1995), p. 81.

[11] Covey, Stephen. *The Seven Habits of Highly Effective People*, (New York: Simon and Schuster, 1989), p. 98.

3

Formulate a Firm Foundation

Once the cost has been counted, many people decide and earnestly desire to make of their lives a temple where the Holy Spirit may dwell. People want to experience the blessings of God and all the benefits appertaining thereto. There is just one essential element lacking. They fail to formulate a firm foundation.

Their theme song is, "I want to be a Christian in my heart."

However, many times they do not want to be a Christian in their behavior, actions, and deeds. Beyond the perusal and scrutiny of society, some people want to do their own thing. They find it difficult to obey God, though professing faith in the Lord.

Persons who tend to have a passing acquaintance with theological parlance argue life today is "under the dispensation of grace," nullifying strict adherence to Divine dictates. One does not have to obey God's commandments because the law is not applicable. Sin is only sin when your trespass is revealed.

Simply stated, these peoples' belief is: "You only sin when you get caught."

We are compelled to differ with such an erroneous and baseless conclusion. Quite the contrary, *obedience is faith's foundation*. Obedience is the groundwork of Christian construction. Anyone who refuses or fails to obey cannot be a mature Christian.

To plead for a faith system which tolerates sinning is to erode and eventually eradicate the ground beneath an effectual faith foundation.

A Jewish thinker, Abraham Joshua Heschel, prolifically makes this point in his work, *God in Search of Man*:

> The world needs more than the secret holiness of individual inwardness. It needs more than sacred sentiments and good intentions. God asks for the heart because He needs the lives. It is by lives that the world will be redeemed, by lives that beat in concordance with God, by deeds that beat out the finite charity of the human heart.[1]

Man's power of action is less vague than his power of intention. An action has intrinsic meaning; its value to the world is independent of what it means to the person performing it. The act of giving food to a helpless child is meaningful regardless of whether or not the moral intention is present. God asks for the heart, and we must spell our answer in terms of deeds.

Albert Edward Day's seminal work, *The Captivating Presence*, treats the issue of obedience. According to Day, obedience is indispensable. What we are called to obey is not a static code, however helpful it may be at times, but obedience to God, Who is present with us in every situation and is speaking to us consistently.

Every obedience, however small (if any obedience is ever small) quickens our sensitivity to Him and our capacity to understand Him and so makes more real our sense of His presence.

The Prophet Samuel, when correcting Israel's first king, gave Saul a word from God, when he disobeyed God yet presumed to take the priest/prophet's role in offering up sacrifices:

> ... Behold, to obey is better than sacrifice, and to hearken than the fat of rams.
>
> For rebellion is as the sin of witchcraft, and stubbornness is as iniquity and idolatry. ...
>
> 1 Samuel 15:22,23

Deuteronomy 5:29 is a reference to God's lamenting the waywardness of His people:

> Oh, that there were such an heart in them, that they would fear me, and keep all my commandments always, that it might be well with them, and with their children for ever!

Jesus is even more illustrative of the foundational premise of obedience in Luke's gospel. He raised a very pertinent and personal question, striking a cord which resounds to the core of disobedience when He asked:

> And why call ye me Lord, Lord, and do not the things which I say?
>
> Luke 6:46

This question was posed at the end of Jesus' teachings on the plain after the disciples had been chosen, but before they had been sent out on a mission. The setting is one of preparation. Jesus has moved from the mountain, a place of prayer, to the plain. He is with his disciples amidst a crowd of people who came from all parts of Judea, Jerusalem, and the coastal region of Tyre and Sidon to hear Him preach and teach and to be cured of their diseases. (Luke 6:17-18.)

Consequently, Jesus was addressing not only his followers (disciples) but all would-be disciples (the people).

Discipleship Demands Work and Sacrifice

The work of discipleship which is for all followers of Jesus does not take place on a mountain summit but in the plain. As Jesus indicated, discipleship demands work and sacrifice.

Samuel Greg (1804-1887) understood well what Jesus was saying here and expressed it in a beautiful hymn:

Stay, Master, stay upon this heavenly hill,
A little longer let us linger still;
With all the mighty ones of old beside,
Near to the awful Presence still abide;
Before the throne of light we trembling stand,
And catch a glimpse into the spirit land.

No, saith the Lord, the hour is past, we go,
Our home, our life, our duties lie below.

While here we kneel upon the mount of prayer,
The plough lies waiting in the furrow there.
Here we sought God that we might know his will;
There we must do it, serve him, seek him still.[2]

In its more immediate context, Jesus has just pointed to the necessity of a firm foundation for discipleship to have integrity. What one is, what one does, what one says are an inseparable union as are a tree and its fruits. Profession of faith must be linked to practice of the same.

> **For a good tree bringeth forth not corrupt fruit; neither doeth a corrupt tree bring forth good fruit.**
>
> **For every tree is known by his own fruit. For of thorns men do not gather figs, nor of a bramble bush gather they grapes.**
>
> **A good man out of the good treasure of his heart bringeth forth that which is good; and an evil man out of the evil treasure of his heart bringeth forth that which is evil: for of the abundance of the heart his mouth speaketh.**
>
> **Luke 6:43-45**

The unforgettable utterance of Jesus that concludes Luke 6 is the commencement as well as the climax of the truth. If my life is to have the stability which Christ can give, it must be built unmistakably in thought and action upon Christ from the beginning. This is true for any individual.

You may have a shallow and reckless notion that you are sufficient unto yourself. It may appear your own life can be constructed on any basis which happens to be easy and agreeable. As long as the weather is fair, such folly may not be evident. But just when you least expect them, here come the floods — the muddy waters of some sudden passion, the rushing current of unforeseen temptation. Because your character has no sure foundation in those principles which loyalty to Christ gives, your whole moral structure may collapse.

Such is also the case for relationships between individuals which ought to be the most precious:

• Friendships cannot be sustained if they are based only on the sands of selfishness.

• Marriages do not endure when they have no ground except physical attraction and have never been undergirded by the deeper loyalties and love that only a consecrated purpose can assure.

Jesus was cognizant of the real or possible danger that some of his followers would speak for Him but not do His words. The real or possible peril is that mere confession of Jesus as Lord when unaccompanied by obedience will not hold one's life during the storms of adversity. As Jesus notes, it is in the storms that a firm foundation is essential.

We want to emphasize, it is in the storms that the difference between interested listeners and loyal obedient disciples will be most evident. An interested listener may attend church, but he will not sell all and give to the poor as an obedient disciple.

The story of Jairus' daughter (Luke 9:1-10) shows that this ruler of the synagogue in his crisis was willing to put his faith in action. He was no mere interested listener. It is not enough to clearly understand and express interest. This is deception of self. (James 1:22-25.) Self-deception will ultimately become self-defeat.

How often have you heard the adage, "First to thine ownself be true?"

That is not what Jesus taught. Jesus required obedience. In fact, obedience to his teachings is the most solid foundation for life. Jesus employed the familiar pedagogical analogous technique to graphically depict the necessity of a firm foundation. He said, in essence, in Luke 6:47,48:

"I will show you what someone is like who comes to me and hears my words and puts them into practice. He is like a man building a house, who digs down deep and lays the foundation on rock. When a flood comes, the torrent strikes that house but cannot shake it, because it is well-built."

Laying a Foundation Is Hard Work

This parable clearly indicates the work ethic of formulating a firm foundation. Obviously, one cannot avoid toil. Admittedly, to dig rock is hard work and much trouble. However, failure to do so in the initial stages of construction is to invite ultimate ruin, disaster, waste, and loss.

There may well be less cumbersome or labor-intensive methods to respond or deal with life's circumstances and situations than Jesus' instructions promise:

You may indeed choose an easier way to handle adversaries or enemies, such as compromise.

You may select options for making money or generating an income which are void of sweat equity, such as illegal distribution of narcotics or fraudulent schemes.

You may pursue avenues to gain an advantage which involves mistreatment of others.

In the end, however, all other choices that do not have obedience to Jesus as a base will perish. "Only what you do for Christ will last."

Ease has ruined far more persons than adversity ever could.

Jesus further elucidated the peril of failing to formulate a firm foundation by giving an account of an individual who opted for ease in construction.

Ease due to hearing Jesus and not doing what he says is tantamount to constructing a house upon the earth without excavation. When the streams flow against such a building, it will immediately fall causing great ruin. What a shame!

One needs to take the long view of life. The long view and the short view involve every decision one needs to make in life.

———————

Happy the person who never barters future good for present pleasure; who sees things not in the light of the moment but in the light of eternity.

———————

Given the critical and indispensable nature of a firm foundation in the construction process, it is essential that one clearly understands the steps involved in laying a foundation that will withstand the inevitable storms of life.

Dr. Konrad Raiser, in an address to the annual meeting of the United States Conference of member churches of the World Council of Churches, stated: "The jubilee signifies the return to the covenant order of God."

According to Raiser, "All the key concepts begin with *re* — repentance, remission, restitution, reparation, restoration, regeneration, recreation, reconstruction, rebuilding, reconciliation."[3]

Repentance Is More Than Being Sorry

Formulating a firm foundation signifies the return to the covenant order of God through Jesus the Christ. The necessary steps are repentance and regeneration. The imperative of repentance was driven home in one writer's mind serendipitously. During a reception amidst the antiquity of Christendom's oldest See, the See of Saint Mark, repentance as the first step along the spiritual trek was underscored.

His Holiness, Pope Shenouda III, 117th Pope and Patriarch of Alexandria, was hosting members of the World Council of Churches Commission on Sharing and Service at his residence in Cairo, Egypt. This sagacious and seemingly indefatigable Patriarch of the Coptic Orthodox Church was pontificating regarding the necessity of sharing resources and servicing marginalized humanity. As his comments concluded in a calm crescendo, His Holiness emphatically stated that repentance is fundamental to spiritual growth.

In effect, this was Protestantism in the presence of an affirming orthodoxy uttering the common ground of repentance as key to nurturing the faith. Regardless of ethic, ethnicity, or ethos, if one is to construct a cathedral of crystal character and conduct, repentance is a must. Any ambition or desire for a mansion in the Master's house can only be fulfilled by repentance.

Repentance is more than being sorry. Metanoia is a more accurate rendition of what is required. It is not a mere turning backward, but a reordering and reorientation that opens the way out of the house of bondage to sin into the household of life unto salvation.

There is the kind of repentance that is regret or remorse – such as being sorry for getting a ticket for speeding. However, the type of repentance that leads to new life is a change of mind resulting in a change of condition, attitudes, and actions. It is an about-face in life. It is an invitation to return to the future, to be liberated from the bonds of the past and to embrace the promise of life.

This echoes the biblical invitation to repentance, interrupting the flow of business as usual and affirming God as the source of life, of wholeness and hope. Instead of the moralizing connotation of repentance, the turning to God suggests a change of allegiance, of liberation from other powers and captivities. This is not an invitation to return to God in the sense of going back, but to turn to the one who is always ahead of us with the promise of true life.

Repentance is not the familiar garb of moralism and religiosity, but a fundamental change in our entire outlook and attitude, a radical reorientation of our lives. This is a new beginning which is like being born again.

The person who repents is one who makes a decision to turn from sin and turn to Jesus as a follower of His. Repentance is the key that unlocks the door to a person's whole lifestyle, so God can work the miracle of the new birth. Repentance is the turning point that directs a person toward God. It is absolutely necessary for a firm foundation. Repentance is one facet but there is another.

Both Repentance and Regeneration Are Required

Regeneration is to repentance what water is to cement in the formulation of a foundation. In order to mix the elements which ultimately formulate the basis for a concrete foundation in the construction process, a builder must have both water and cement. Any person desiring to be a Christian must repent and be regenerated. One without the other is not sufficient to formulate a firm foundation on which to construct a Christian life.

We propose now to display, as clearly as possible, the nature of regeneration and the means by which it is accomplished. A clear distinction between regeneration and other experiences of the spiritual life is not always maintained.

Regeneration implies a radical change, which revolutionizes our whole being, contradicts and overcomes our old fallen nature, and places us into a state of reverence, confidence, and obedience to God. It is God's will for all men to be made partakers of this new life.

Hence, God requires all men to repent and turn unto Him before He will or can effect regeneration.

A firm foundation for spiritual growth consists of repentance and faith in Christ, which is the response on our part that leads to the Divine act of regeneration or renewal. God's Spirit enters into union with the believing, accepting spirit of man.

Allow us to emphasize that regeneration is not the completion of construction in itself. Rather, regeneration is the starting point of spiritual growth. Regeneration is a component in formulating a firm foundation.

The operative word in characterizing regeneration is change. The principle characteristic of regeneration is a change of heart from a state of carelessness about God to loyalty towards Him. This causes one to follow after duty with a passion and appetite.

Regeneration is a change from being preoccupied with pleasing the flesh. There is an end to possessive instincts. Property is acquired and held, not for self-aggrandizement but for beneficent activity and useful abundant living. All things are changed into a means for the highest good in a solemn preparation to serve God and humanity.

The whole object of life is changed. Natural abilities, whose balance inclines towards the selfish nature, are reversed or changed and all faculties bend toward God. The soul is made to sing, "I know I've been changed, the Angels in heaven have changed my name."

Finally, the regenerate state is characterized by a new morality. The measure of an individual is morality and not learning. Be the world's measurement what it may, this is the measurement of the Great Architect and Inspector! The Great Inspector will grant a certificate of occupancy according to the manner in which an individual meets His moral measurement or falls short of it. Based on the outcome, God will reward or punish in eternity.

The process of how regeneration is accomplished is outside our observation and beyond the scope of analysis. It takes place in the sphere of subconsciousness. In the words of H.E. Warner, "Here God works in the depth of the soul as silently and securely as if on the remotest world of the Stellar universe."[4]

Truthfully, the agent by whom regeneration is made possible is none other than the Holy Spirit. This is the motive power of a regenerated life, ultimately. The twin essentials of repentance and regeneration combine to concretize a foundation to withstand the wind and waves of adversity – a foundation illustrative of a line from the early American melody:

> How firm a foundation, ye saints of the Lord,
> Is laid for your faith in His excellent Word!
> What more can He say than to you He hath said,
> To you who for refuge to Jesus have fled?

Endnotes

[1]Heschel, Abraham Joshua. *God in Search of Man*, (New York: Octagon Books, 1972), p. 288.

[2]Gregg, Samuel. "Stay, Master, Upon This Heavenly Hill." *Methodist Hymn Book*, (London: Methodist Publishing House, 1954), p. 223.

[3]Raiser, Dr. Konrad. "An Ecumenical Jubilee: What It Might Mean For The Churches." (Geneva, Switzerland: 1995), p. 6.

[4]Orr, James, Ed. *The International Standard Bible Encyclopedia*, (Grand Rapids: Wm. B. Eerdman's Publishing Co., 1956), p. 2550.

4

Comply With the Specifications

The construction of Christian character is not a coincidental consequence stumbled onto through trial and error or mere experience. One could argue experience is a good teacher.

To such a claim Minna Atrim retorts, "Experience is a good teacher but she runs up big bills."[1]

When sustenance of sanity and the survival of the soul is at stake, bills accumulated through experience may be too much to pay.

What perhaps could be fatal flaws in construction may be avoided by following the plans or specifications established by an architect. Every builder or contractor must be aware of what specifications are to be complied with prior to commencing work. Failure to know the standard results in non-compliance. This will incur the displeasure of the inspector when the building is complete.

Jesus is unambiguous about the requirements for becoming Christian, as one cannot be held accountable for that which he does not know. Each person who is under construction as a Christian must be cognizant of the Master's specifications for constructing an acceptable Christian life.

These standards must be known and conformed to in order for Him to compliment you with the words, "Well done, good and faithful servant." (Matt. 25:21.) Failure to perform that which is known has harsh consequences.

One has to be cautious about how he conducts himself based on societal standards as opposed to those of the Saviour. Substitutes are often utilized in today's world and passed off as authentic and just as qualitative as the authentic product:

Nylon has been substituted for silk.

Margarine is used for butter.

Sugar substitutes are very profitable.

As it relates to the proclamation of the gospel, earnestness may be readily and without detection substituted or mistaken for unction,[2] as well as a number of substitutes presented for genuine salvation.

In an attempt to explain what we perceive genuine salvation to be, we will say just a word about what it is not. We will proceed from a negative to reach a positive. To state it another way, we will state several common misconceptions about salvation in an effort to clarify salvific specifications, concepts that are not salvation:

1. *Service is not salvation.* To do good deeds is quite laudable and commendable, but it is not indicative of salvation. Humanitarianism is not to be equated with Christianity. One can be a humanitarian and not Christian, but one cannot be Christian and not a humanitarian. There is an often-used adage which reminds us of this point.

Being good will keep you out of jail,

But only God can prevent you from going to Hell!

---

2. *Salvation is not turning over a new leaf.* You can not be saved by simply reforming your ways and saying, "I will clean up my life, and start over again."

Isaiah 64:6 reminds us,

But we are all as an unclean thing, and all our righteousnesses are as filthy rags; and we all do fade as a leaf; and our iniquities, like the wind, have taken us away.

3. *Salvation is not maintaining proper cerebration.* Stated the other way around, right thinking is not salvation. A modern gnosticism[3] is to be avoided at all cost. It is not thinking lofty, amorphous, and esoteric thoughts. The base, fallen nature of human beings limits our capacity to truly conceive high thoughts.

4. *Salvation is not cultivating and concentrating on a "divine spark" within each of us*, as New Agers claim. Man is not born "good," then becomes "bad" through societal influences.

5. *Self-denial is not salvation.* Heathens master the art of all types of asceticism. Crucifying yourself physically is not sufficient to save you. The object is not to prove to yourself or others your ability to accomplish difficult and masochistic feats.

6. *Not even sacrifice is salvation.* The supreme sacrifice of dying for a great cause is not salvific. A

martyr mentality is no more meaningful or marvelous than mere morality. A person can not be cleansed from sin through discipline alone. Paying for his own, or even someone else's, wrongdoing does not a Christian make.

Jesus Did What He Told Us To Do

Consider the specifications laid out by the Christ. The Master does not require us to do what He failed to consistently do during His journey upon earth. He commanded, **Follow me, and I will make you fishers of men** (Matt. 4:19b).

His is a record of personal contact from beginning to end. From the time He initially called the disciples, saying to Andrew, "Come and see," (John 1:39) until He assured the penitent thief, "Today you will be with Me in paradise" (Luke 23:43), ultimately He was in touch with people.

He was cogent and clear about God's plan of salvation. As a Christian, whether to follow the plan is not optional. Failure to do so is an exercise in futility as one begins the quest to become Christian. According to Albert Edward Day, humans attempting to work out their salvation alone are a pathetic spectacle — hopelessly defeated moralists trying to elevate themselves by their own bootstraps.

Jesus packaged all there is to becoming Christian in a nice neat blueprint. A scribe, obviously impressed with Jesus' adroit handling of His critic's inquiries, asked which of the ten commandments was greatest. The question the scribe asked was an honest one. In some respects his question is the most fundamental question of the faith. This query was really seeking a succinct statement of the primary aim of one's existence.

In answering Jesus drew on His knowledge of tradition and quoted from the "Shema," a Jewish statement of faith found in Deuteronomy 6:4, **Hear, O Israel: The Lord our God is one Lord.**

This verse is an affirmation of monotheism, the belief in one God, which necessitates an inherent duality of relationship, the manifestation of which is both vertical and horizontal. Horizontal harmony is predicated upon vertical veracity.

Jesus summed up the vertical dimension that every would-be Christian must comply with: Love the Lord your God with the entirety of heart, soul, mind, and strength. God is to be *a priori*[4] in our lives. He alone is to have the supreme place. No other love can be allowed to rival love for God. (See Chapter One.)

Simply stated, this means a person's first obligation is to love God with the totality of being. The heart speaks of the emotional nature, the soul of the volitional nature, the mind of the intellectual nature, and the strength of the physical nature.

Then Jesus specified the horizontal regulation and responsibility. One is to love one's neighbor as oneself. We are to love God more than self and our neighbor as self. Thus, the life that really matters is concerned with God first, then with others. Material things are not even mentioned. Only God and people are significant.

Barnes says:

> Love to God and man comprehends the whole of religion: and to produce this has

been the design of Moses, the prophets, the Saviour, and the apostles.[5]

We should ponder this dual demand laid down by Jesus. Then we must strive to do it. We are not permitted to say to others, "Do as I say, but not as I do." Such a statement serves to undermine the credibility of our profession of faith. The unsaved must see practitioners of the faith in order to have a clear picture of Jesus. We cannot pretend. God knows our hearts and others may perceive our motives.

Love of God and neighbor is far more important than rituals. People can perform religious ceremonies and put on a public display of piety without inward, personal holiness. God is concerned about what a person is inwardly as well as outwardly.

True Christians do not attempt to deceive God, others, or self with superfluous external religion. Realizing that God looks on the heart, true believers hasten to Him for cleansing from sin and for power to live in a manner pleasing in His sight.

Loving One's Neighbor Is the Hard Part

Practically speaking, people sometimes find it difficult to comply with this relational mandate. They may adhere to the vertical but not the horizontal. In society, it is not uncommon to see professing Christians opposed to others because of a difference in race, creed, color, or sexual orientation. These attitudes are still prevalent in today's world.

Recently, during a visit to South Africa, the vestiges of apartheid were still very visible. People continue to live in enclaves demarcated along racial and even tribal lines.

Even in this country, the so-called "land of the free and home of the brave," atrocities against others are perpetrated in the name of God. Such realizations make it obvious that there is a distortion in our understanding of what is required by the Architect regarding relationships with others.

Modern Christians seem to have the mind-set that their only consideration should be how to relate to God.

We forget that the depth of the vertical is determined in large measure by the breadth of the horizontal.

The reverberating cord is found in Matthew 25:41:

> **. . . Inasmuch as ye did it unto one of the least of these my brethren, ye have done it unto me.**

How can one profess love for a God they have never seen, but cannot treat the people whom they can see with mutual respect?

Then there are those who seem to do well on the horizontal plane, but falter with the vertical. This is evident in the philanthropic humanitarian who trivializes the necessity of what Martin Buber terms an "I-Thou relationship." These people seem to have little problem with being kind and polite. Others say nice things about them.

Their deeds are benevolent and beneficial. What they do is the right thing. Yet, they do the right thing for the wrong reason. Their actions are not compelled by a God-consciousness. Motives for proper behavior range from societal expectation to tax evasion through contributing to charitable organizations.

This is indicative of a misunderstanding of what it means to become Christian. Often the impression is given that being "good" equates with becoming Christian. Being good may well meet the norm for staying out of jail, but only God can keep a person out of hell. This is a saying which should not be taken lightly. It should never be forgotten that only what is done for Christ will last.

The late African-American pulpiteer and orator of great note, Martin Luther King, Jr., spoke to this relational issue in a homily entitled, "The Dimensions of a Complete Life." He structured his argument around Revelation 21:16. This scriptural passage comments on the Holy City to come down out of Heaven that, "its length, breadth, and height are equal."

King argued, in analogy, that the *length* of life is what you do for yourself; the *breadth* is what one does for others; and ultimately, the *height* of life is what you do for God.

Knowledge of God's will as it is revealed in Scripture places on the would-be Christian great responsibility to adhere to it. Much has been given to us, and much will be required of us. Worse still is what results when one knows the standard but fails to act upon what is known. The consequences for non-compliance are as clear as the specifications themselves.

The person who knows his Master's will and does not comply with the same shall be beaten with many stripes, according to Luke 12:47. We are commanded to do that which we have seen and heard.

> **Therefore, my beloved brethren, be ye stedfast, unmoveable, always abounding in the work of the Lord, forasmuch as ye know that your labour is not in vain in the Lord.**

Corinthians 15:58

Endnotes

[1] Atrim, Minna.

[2] Bounds, E.M. *The Complete Works of E.M. Bounds on Prayer*, (Grand Rapids: Baker Book House, 1990), p. 479.

[3] *Gnosticism* was a movement that became very well known in the third century as a mixture of Greek philosophy, Oriental mysticism, and some elements of Christianity. It taught salvation through knowledge, and has made a come back in the late-20th century in some of the New Age groups.

[4] *A priori* means "from cause to effect, or from a generalization to a particular instance," or "reasoning deductively," according to Webster's *New World Dictionary*, (New York: Simon & Schuster, 1980), p. 68.

[5] McDonald, William. *Believer's Bible Commentary*, (Nashville: Thomas Nelson Publishers, Inc., 1940), p. 1288.

5

The Elevation of Imagination

Unless the human spirit is challenged for the pursuit of greatness through lofty ideals and benevolent practice it may aimlessly meander in a maze of mediocrity. Humanism and secularism can rob the soul of its true identity. The Christian was not intended to be a pawn in Faust's chess game of life.[1]

Indeed, in John 1:11,12, we find the standard aspiration of every would-be Christian:

He came unto his own, and his own received him not.

But as many as received him, to them gave he power to become the sons (children) of God, even to them that believe on his name.

He gave *power to become.* There are those who contend that this is the most encouraging phrase in the Bible. No matter what you have been or who you are, when you become a child of God, you are given "power to become."

———————————

A familiar story is told about two young explorers who discovered an unattended egg while mountain climbing. Aware that it belonged to a bird, they took the egg home and placed it under a brooding hen. When the egg hatched, it was noticeably different than the other chicklets in the coop. Yet day by day, month by month, it fluttered and pecked clumsily around the barnyard like its companions.

One day a majestic eagle soared over the barnyard, its mighty pinions casting a shadow upon the beak and brow of this misidentified eaglet. Instantly, something stirred within its bosom. It fluttered haplessly around and finally climbed and sputtered to the roof of the chicken coop, stretched forth its wings and leaped toward the vaulted sky. It ascended up toward the snow-capped mountain, up into the air.

Something was awakened in that eagle that said, "You are more than what you have become."[2]

John 1:11,12 gives us a glimpse into the mind and motive of the Master in regards to human redemption. Who were His own?

Was this a veiled attempt at nationalism?

Was the writer speaking ethnically, biologically, sociologically or anthropologically?

Was it an issue of blood rights?

All of those questions may be answered "no." The context clearly reveals that in the natural, blood may be "thicker than water," but biblically, the spirit is thicker than blood. Or, rather, the blood of Jesus which binds all true Christians together is "thicker" — more final and lasting — than natural ties of any kind. The blood ties of those in the family of God are eternal.

We may be "hatched" with the chickens, but we are "born again" as eaglets.

The scripture reads **for as many as believed on him**, or received Him. That sounds remarkably similar to "whosoever." Whether male or female; rich or poor; black, white or any shade between; whether well-educated or illiterate, Jew or Gentile, if the requisite belief was attained, He gave them "power to become." (Gal. 3:28,29.)

Newly constructed Christians must not view themselves as mere "drawers of water and hewers of wood" (Josh. 9:21), or as we might say today, "megabytes in Cyberspace." Their estimations and imaginations of themselves must be elevated to the position of royalty. It is they who become the "children of God." They do not — as Descartes would suggest — "think, therefore they are,"[3] but they *believe* their way into family-hood.

Merrill C. Tenney comments on this passage,

> Just as there is a sharp antithesis in vv. 4-5 between darkness and light, so here is an equally direct contrast between rejection and reception. In spite of the many who rejected the Word, there were some who received him. This provides the initial definition of *believe* by equating it with *receive*. When we accept a gift, whether tangible or intangible, we thereby demonstrate our confidence in its reality and trustworthiness. . . . "Become" indicates

clearly that people are not spiritual children of God by natural birth, for we cannot become what we already are.[4]

Does it take great power to become? The Greek linguists define power in at least six ways. *Dunamis* (mighty), *exousia* (right), *ischus* (ability), *kratos* (strength), *arche* (rule), and *dunaton* (powerful).[5] In the text with which we are dealing, the term is more accurately defined as "right." Hence, believing and receiving give access to family status.

To some, such a distinction would appear to be an exercise in redundancy. After all, we are all created by the will of God. There is however a difference between being a creation of God and a child of God. Membership has its privileges. The children of God have the Spirit of Christ operating in their lives in three dimensions, thus insuring that constructed Christians will be more than casual Christians.

Three Dimensions of the Spirit

Christ in you

The great 19th-century, British pastor/preacher, Charles Haddon Spurgeon, in reflecting on Colossians 1:27 [**Christ in you the hope of glory**], wrote that this sentence reads like a "whole body of divinity condensed into one line."[6] It provides a blessed assurance of internal resolve amidst the machinations of a menacing world. Christ within prompts the fainting and faltering soul to reach "higher, higher."

There is no substitute for the presence of Christ in one's life.

Spurgeon also told a story of a man afflicted with a terminal disease who went to be treated by a physician who specialized in curing his condition. When he arrived at the office the doctor was not in. The man prepared to wait until he returned, but the clerk informed him that he need not wait, because the doctor's assistant was there.

The man replied, "I don't care about the assistant. I want to see the doctor. Mine is a desperate case."

The clerk confirmed that the doctor was out, but his books were there to be consulted. The man replied that the books would not do. The industrious clerk then pointed out that the cabinet with all of the doctor's medicine was there, but again, the man replied, "They will not do."

Finally the clerk said, "Here is one who has been cured by the doctor, surely he can help." However, the man responded, "The evidence of one who has been helped by him is all the more reason that I must see the doctor myself."[7]

There is no substitute for the abiding presence of Christ in you. No text, no testimony, no teacher, no tonic can adequately serve as an elixir for the soul.

Christ with you

This does not invoke the interpretation of Immanuel. That name means (deity) *God (incarnate) with us.* It supports the Christological construct that God took on flesh and "dwelt among us."

In chapter 14 of the fourth Gospel, Jesus offered assurance to His timid and tempted disciples that He would abide with them forever through the Comforter (*Paracletos*), which is interpreted "another like the other," or "one who comes alongside to help."[8] There is a dynamic that occurs as a result of a shared experience which encourages the heart to be strong in life's most demanding situations.

Stephen's beatific vision (Acts 7:55,56), Paul's serenity in shipwreck (Acts 20), and John on the Isle of Patmos in the Spirit (Rev. 1:1) all confirm the contention of the psalmist long years before:

> **Yea, though I walk thru the valley of the shadow of death, I will fear no evil: for thou art with me; thy rod and thy staff they comfort me.**
>
> **Psalm 23:4**

The words of the well-known hymn are a recapitulation of David's theme in Psalm 23:

There's not a friend like the lowly Jesus.
No, not one!
   No, not one!

None else can heal our soul's diseases, No not one!
   No not one!

Jesus knows all about our struggles, He will guide till the day is done.

There's not a friend like the lowly Jesus.
No, not one!
   No, not one!"

Christ for you

The first Epistle of John says, . . . **If any man sin, we have an advocate with the Father, Jesus Christ the righteous** (1 John 2:1).

An *advocate* is one who speaks for another, who supports and defends.[9] The necessity of such heavenly favor is acutely felt when one considers the ferocity of the adversary.

> **Be sober, be vigilant; because your adversary the devil, as a roaring lion, walketh about, seeking whom he may devour.**
>
> **1 Peter 5:8**

As a Christian succumbs to the subtle seductions of the adversary, the Advocate comes to his or her aid, and not simply to defend at the adjudication. On the contrary, contrite Christians need a reassuring and reviving word when sin has entered their domain. They need not remain in the grip of guilt and shame, but can regain their rightful place and responsibility in the Kingdom's community.

Christ's approval provides the Christian with self-esteem, self-worth, self-love, and self-affirmation. Theologians would refer to this as a *numinouos* experience.[10] Creative imaging begins the metamorphosing process within the Christian's spirit.

> Consider the lowly caterpillar. It is self-evident that the caterpillar and butterfly live in entirely different worlds . . . the caterpillar can fly but not as a caterpillar — only as a butterfly.[11]

The knowledge and assurance that we are the children of God eliminates the predisposition of low-living, sight-walking, small-thinking, and negative-speaking. We are being conformed to the image of God.

A man who had not seen his brother for a number of years went to the airport to pick him up for a visit. After a period of waiting and watching, he began walking toward a disembarking passenger. He called out his name, and the brothers embraced.

Someone asked, "How did you recognize your brother so quickly?"

He replied, "I knew he was my brother *because he walked like my father.*"[12] Can we be recognized because we walk like our Father?

Dr. Maxwell Maltz, noted plastic surgeon and author, explored the impact reconstructive surgery can have on the attitude and aspirations of many of his patients in a book entitled, *New Faces, New Futures.*[13] In like manner, one could contend, "New Faith, New Future" or "New Family (of God), New Future."

Within the expanse of free moral agency, God gives each person a choice and each Christian the "power to become."

Lord lift us up where we belong . . . where the eagle flies!

Endnotes

[1] Wolfgang. *Faust*, (New York: The Modern ...ouse, 1950). Faust is the leading character who ... ith Mephistopheles (the devil) in this 1808 tragedy-drama.

[2] Mufasa to Semba in Walt Disney Pictures' *The Lion King*.

[3] Rene Descartes, a French philosopher who lived in the late 16th and early 17th centuries taught (in a nutshell) that man exists because he thinks.

[4] Gaebelein, Frank, Gen. Ed. *The Expositor's Bible Commentary*, (Grand Rapids: Zondervan Publishing Co., 1981), p. 32.

[5] Vine, W.E. *Vine's Expository Dictionary of New Testament Words*, (McLean, VA: MacDonald Publishing House, 1981), pp. 898,899.

[6] Spurgeon, C.H. "Christ in You," *Metropolitan Tabernacle Pulpit Series*, 1883, p. 265.

[7] Ibid.

[8] Vine's.

[9] *Webster's New Dictionary and Roget's Thesaurus*, (Nashville: Thomas Nelson Publishers, 1984), p. 10.

[10] Strong, James. *Strong's Exhaustive Concordance*, (Grand Rapids: Baker Book House, 1982).

[11] Butterfield, Eric. *Discover the Power Within You*, (San Francisco: Harper & Row Publishers, 1968), p. 23.

[12] Maxwell, John C. *Your Attitude: Key to Success,* Here's Life Publishers, 1984, p. 41.

[13] Maltz, Dr. Maxwell. *New Faces, New Futures*, (New York: Simon and Schuster, 1960), p. 80.

6
Examine the Entrance

In this pluralistic, complex, global community where the accessibility to information abounds, we find ourselves bombarded with doctrinal polemics, dogmatic pronouncements, and prophetic promises for pragmatic prosperity without any painful perils or problems. As a result we are presented with alternatives, options, choices.

The paramount question becomes which route should one pursue?

Among those persons pointing to the path through preachments and pedagogy, who is most accurate and authentic?

What are the visible characteristics or signs which indicate the correct course?

Which is the proper portal to pass through?

Responding to these concerns is perhaps the most difficult task of all. Initially, it may seem there are a multiplicity of choices competing for attention, with each offering its own set of benefits and blessings.

A word of caution is necessary up front. Be extremely careful about rushing into anything too hastily. A series of clichés, that may be hackneyed but are still true, are helpful to emphasize this caveat:

- Fools rush in where angels fear to tread!

- All that glitters is not gold!

- Things are not always as they seem!

- However, nothing ventured, nothing gained! But tread lightly!

Be certain to examine the entrance before going in. This involves "looking before you leap." It is strongly recommended the investigation entail more than a cursory look. The best advice is to scrutinize the opening prior to entry. Painstaking attention to detail ought be given.

Though there seem to be numerous entrances from which to select, that is not the case. "Selection" always suggests that one may choose from several things. However, as it relates to the entrance into the faith, there is only one choice.

Each individual must choose between one of two alternatives. The emphasis is on the act of a free will exercised in making the decision and on the finality of the same.

There is no compulsion. No one is going to push or shove you through the door. The choice is yours.

Poetically, an aged Robert Frost in graphic nostalgic fashion wrote a well-known poem that is illustrative of the choice which confronts us and the decisive difference it makes.

"The Road Not Taken"

Two roads diverged in a yellow wood,
And sorry I could not travel both
And be one traveler, long I stood
And looked down one as far as I could
To where it bent in the undergrowth;

Then took the other, as just as fair,
And having perhaps the better claim,
Because it was grassy and wanted wear;
Though as for that, the passing there
Had worn them really about the same,

And both that morning equally lay
In leaves no step had trodden black.
Oh, I kept the first for another day!
Yet knowing how way leads on to way,
I doubted if I should ever come back.

I shall be telling this with a sigh
Somewhere ages and ages hence:
Two roads diverged in a wood,
And I took the one less traveled by,
And that has made all the difference.[1]

Frost's poem suggests an almost exilic, exclusive existence. It is obvious that only few venture down the grassy path. This poem has an icy impact upon us mere mortals. According to psychiatrist Abraham Maslow, once our basic needs for sustenance, security, and shelter are met, our next highest need is to find favor with the crowd.

How does such a desire get fulfilled when one walks along the road less traveled?

Thomas Jefferson believed and wrote that the will of the majority should prevail.

If in fact that is the case, why not choose the entrance based on the political principle of majority rule? After all, we do live in a "democratic" society, although this country was founded as a Republic. Besides, who wants to walk alone void of human companionship?

Cebes of antiquity, a disciple of Socrates, gives us a philosophical note on this subject:

> Seest thou not a certain small door, and a pathway before the door, in no way crowded, for only few travel that way, since it seems to lead through a pathless, rugged, and strong tract? That is the way that leadeth to true discipline.[2]

The definitive word on this matter is neither Frost's poetry, Jefferson's political thinking, or Cebes' philosophy. Rather it is contained in the pedagogy of Jesus.

Jesus Showed Us Only Two Ways to Travel

In the seventh chapter of Matthew's gospel, Jesus' Sermon on the Mount reaches a crescendo with verse 12:

> **Therefore all things what soever ye would that men should do to you, do ye even so to them: for this is the law and the prophets.**

What follows is a series of practical warnings, the last of which we mentioned earlier (See Chapter 2), to encourage the disciples to adhere to the core teachings within the discourse.

Jesus was attempting to impress on the hearers the distinction between real and nominal discipleship. This parabolic message is not pessimistic but realistic. Employing the dipartite metaphor, once again, the Master admonishes:

> Enter by the narrow gate; for wide is the gate and broad is the way that leads to destruction, and there are many who go in by it.
>
> Because narrow is the gate and difficult is the way which leads to life, and there are few who find it.
>
> Matthew 7:13-14

In this message, Jesus seems to be sanctioning the philosophical thought of Cebes and the poetic point of Frost. Now what are we to do? It is essential we take with utter seriousness our responsibility to do what is right. The call is for wholehearted commitment to Jesus and denouncement of spurious discipleship.

Jesus spoke of two ways which lie before people. He made it crystal clear there are two ways in life — and only two — which confront all people. Thusly, it is imperative the right choice be made.

This pericope on the two ways is not included in the synoptic gospels. However, the imagery of two ways leading to diametrically opposed goals is not novel but can be found in ancient Scripture and in Jewish writings. The Essenes of Qumran also contrasted the way of light and the way of darkness.

The metaphor is used in Deuteronomy 30 and Jeremiah 21, contrasting the way of life and the way of death.

> I call heaven and earth to record this day against you, that I have set before you life and death, blessing and cursing: therefore choose life, that both thou and thy seed may live.
>
> That thou mayest love the Lord thy God, and that thou mayest obey his voice, and that thou mayest cleave unto him: for he is thy life, and the length of thy days: that thou mayest dwell in the land which the Lord sware unto thy fathers, to Abraham, to Isaac, and to Jacob, to give them.

Deuteronomy 30:19,20

> And unto this people thou shalt say, Thus saith the Lord; Behold, I set before you the way of life, and the way of death.

Jeremiah 21:8

In the first psalm, the way of the righteous and the way of the wicked also are contrasted:

> For the Lord knoweth the way of the righteous: but the way of the ungodly shall perish.

Psalm 1:6

The Deuteronomic passage depicts the Israelites standing on the boundary of the land of promise as Joshua addresses them. They were about to accept the offer of life on the land God was giving them. Before they did, they were explicitly confronted with a choice. To choose life and thereby live within the covenant or choose death by living in disobedience to the covenant.

In Psalm 1, the psalmist claims that each way of life has its own distinct destiny. He expressly warns, as does Jesus in Matthew 5-7, that the outcome of life depends on one's guidance by God's Torah (Law).

Emil Bruner accurately stated:

Jesus began his sermon with unqualified tenderness, embracing in the Blessings those who felt least embraceable. He concludes with unqualified toughness, warning us that his sermon is not an intellectual option, a set of suggestions we may take or leave, one philosophy among several others, but that it is the exclusive way to life.[3]

Jesus began His discourse on the two ways with a firm command, "Enter," though at this juncture He does not reveal what gate is in mind. He only says it is narrow. Not until the climax of this saying are we informed it is the way into life. A narrow gate must be sought out. One can not perceive it as readily as the broad gate.

The implication is that something of an effort must be made to enter the narrow gate — for there is another which is more easily perceived. By contrast, there is a gate that is broad and a road that is spacious. A number of the words and metaphors in these verses require closer scrutiny.

The *New Revised Version* of the Bible contains **the way is easy**, but this is inaccurate and misleading. Jesus was not referring to ease of passage but commodiousness, a road on which many might be found.

This scenario has the broad road leading to a splendid gate which is obvious and clearly seen, whereas the path that brings the traveler to the unpretentious gate is inconspicuous and difficult to see. Only those who search for it carefully can see this narrow gate.

Someone wrote that the road to destruction is paved with good intentions. This is the commodious road which leads to destruction, a fact its popularity does nothing to alter. Popularity simply means many go through this gate.

The word *many* as utilized here does not refer to outsiders, unbelievers, Jewish opponents, but to insiders, disciples who begin to follow but go through the wrong gate. They may be swept in by the crowd or the desire to find favor with them. Few also is used similarly. Both words carry a hortatory function.

"Narrow" brings us back to the right gate and exclaims its small dimensions. In contrast to the broad gate, this one is narrow. In contrast to the spacious road, this one is constricted. Though narrow and superficially less attractive than the broad road, this path leads to life.

"Life" often refers to life in a physical sense, this mundane, mortal, existential existence. The reference in this context is obviously to the fuller and more satisfying life, which Christ alone brings about, eternal life.

Few Find the Narrow Path

Few find this path. This is not surprising for the vast majority of people do not receive Jesus' message. Disciples are reminded here that the way to life involves misunderstanding, rejection, and persecution. Those who strive to do what is right must not expect popular acclaims (I Pet. 4:4).

Regardless of how many are seen going along the broad road, it is significant to choose the narrow way. No one drifts into the narrow way by chance. Though the way which leads to life is demanding, it is not discouraging. There is unspeakable joy and fulfillment in discovering this path to life.

A familiar colloquial phrase in the first person, which is also the title of a Southern gospel song, affirms the joy by emphatically declaring, "I wouldn't take nothin' for my journey now!"

After making it clear that those on the narrow way are comparatively few to others who prefer the commodious path, Jesus hastened to warn of those who would help or hinder one's choosing the proper portal of entry. He further cautioned about people who can be depended on to advocate the wrong way in some shape, form, or fashion.

Then, as now, it behooves those who seek *the way* to beware of those who claim falsely to speak in the name of God. People of God have never lacked false teachers or prophets whose emphasis is to lead them away from God.

Recently, a woman who lost her husband of twenty years in death shared her story. She had been reared in the Hindu faith but converted to Christianity upon marriage. This mother of two college students witnessed the death of her spouse at 44 years old as they played squash together.

Following the husband's untimely demise, she had difficulty reconciling the notion of a caring, compassionate God who would permit such a devastating act. In her hurt and pain, she encountered a cult or sect which deified a human who appeared to perform miracles. He spread ashes among his followers and passed out trinkets and ornaments.

The cult seemed to have been growing in popularity. Persons of all sorts and status were flocking to the meetings. She described her interest as mere intrigue.

Jesus addressed this issue by telling us to beware of those who are deceptively clad, presenting themselves as harmless. False prophets do not have to be sought out but prey upon the casual disciple.

They appear "in clothing of sheep," the most submissive of all animals. In reality, they are ravenous wolves, animals with insatiable appetites inwardly differentiating their essential nature from their outward appearance. (Matt. 7:15.)

Jesus was referring to religious teachers ("false prophets") who put on a benevolent front to deceive and destroy. They pretend to be leading one through the gate to greener pastures and still waters. However, their real interest is self-aggrandizement and profit for self.

Sheep they may appear to be, but remember the earlier cliche, "Things are not always what they seem." Their inward character indicates they will always be wolves who try to further their own interest at the expense of those of the flock.

How can those who follow the Christ recognize fraudulent fingers who pretend to point the way?

The fruits of false prophets will in the end betray them. *Fruit* is figuratively used in the Bible for a variety of produce. Here it is stressed that the proof is in the product not the appearance.

Examine the Fruit

Disciples should take note of what these false prophets do and refuse to be charmed by what they say. It is well said, "People would rather see a good sermon than to hear one any day." Often people cannot hear what is said for watching what is done.

As it was for Joshua with the Israelites, the psalmist with the way of the righteous and wicked, so it is for Jesus and His disciples then and now. We are constantly confronted with the choice between life and death, the way of wickedness and righteousness, right and wrong, light and dark, and the narrow and broad way. Examination of the entrance is all about choices.

John Oxenham poetically describes these choices:

> To every man there openeth
> A way and ways and a way:
> And the high soul climbs the high way
> And the low soul gropes the low;
> And in between on the misty flats
> The rest drift to and fro;
> But to every man there openeth
> A high way and a low;
> And every man decideth
> The way his soul must go.[4]

It is not sufficient to think as others think, and do as others do. We must not be satisfied to follow the fashion and swim with the stream of those among whom we live.

These are terrifying truths! Those who hear them ought to diligently search their hearts:

Which way am I going?

On what road am I traveling?

We are all journeying along one way or the other. May God grant us an honest search light of the soul to show us where and what we are!

We may have cause to tremble and be fearful if our religion is that of the multitude. If we can only say, "We do as others do, we go where they go, worship as others worship and hope we will do as well as others at last," we are literally pronouncing our own condemnation.

This is no more than being in the broad way. What is this but being on the road whose end is *destruction*? Such a religion is not presently a saving religion. There is no reason to be cast down and discouraged if the religion we profess and practice is not popular and few agree with us. We must remember the words of our Lord Jesus the Christ, "Narrow is the gate." Repentance, faith in Christ and holiness of life have never been fashionable. The true flock of Christ has always been small.

If we are considered fanatical, peculiar, strange and narrow, we must not become alarmed. This is the narrow road. Surely it is better to enter into life everlasting with a few, than to go to destruction with many. Even when one chooses the proper portal of entry, there is a chance for deviation. It is easy to stray from the path of righteousness. Therefore, we now turn our attention to how one can return to a right relationship with God should he or she stumble.

Endnotes

[1]Frost, Robert. *Poetry and Prose*, "The Road Not Taken," (New York: Holt, Rinehart, and Winston, 1972), p. 16.

[2]*The Interpreter's Bible Commentary*, Vol. 7, (Nashville: Abingdon Press, 1979), pp. 330,331.

[3]Bruner, Emil. *The Divine Imperative* (Philadelphia: Westminster Press, 1947), p. 282.

[4]Oxenham, John. *Literacy: Writing, Reading, and Social Organisation*, (London: Routledge and Kegan, 1980).

7

The Reparation of a Reputation

Despite the best efforts of pro-family lobbies and prohibitive preachments, there appears to be an insatiable appetite within society for scandalous and (scurrilous) seedy information. Each week millions of readers patronize periodicals the likes of *The National Enquirer, Star Magazine, The Globe, The National Examiner,* to name a few, in an attempt to satisfy that hunger.

For those who have an aversion to reading, "tabloid television" appeases their palate's desire. Serendipitous encounters occur in the White House, the courthouse, the statehouse, the jailhouse and even the church house. What adds injury to insult is that Christians seem to enjoy knowing about it, hearing about it, reading about it and talking about it.

Many persons caught in the web of seduction, scandal, and sin refer to themselves as Christians. The question before us is:

Can a reputation be repaired?

Can a weather-beaten Christian be remodeled, remolded, and rehabilitated into a structure of dignity, distinction, and destiny?

A fascinating narrative is recorded in the gospel of John 8:1-11, which reads in part:

> **And the scribes and Pharisees brought unto him a woman taken in adultery; and when they had set her in the midst.**
>
> **They say unto him, Master, this woman was taken in adultery, in the very act.**
>
> **Now Moses in the law commanded us, that such should be stoned; but what sayest thou?**
>
> **John 8:3-6**

Talk about a reputation in need of repair! Caught in "the very act"! Before we extrapolate eternal truths that exude from this exposition, it is important to acknowledge the opposition of some biblical scholars to this pericope of scripture. Scholars justifiably argue that this narrative is not found in most of the early copies of the gospel. Merrill C. Tenney expresses the sentiment of many authors, however:

> To say that it does not belong in the Gospel is not identical with rejecting it as unhistorical. Its coherence and spirit show that it was preserved from a very early time, and it accords well with the known character of Jesus.[1]

Like Tenney, and scores of others, we believe this narrative fits within "a *locus classicus* of Johannine theology."[2] In this text one sees Jesus exceeding the Rogerian notion of "unconditional positive regard," where He looks beyond a person's faults and sees their need.

Jesus spoke to Christians through the ages in this encounter: "Regardless of how spotted your past, your future is spotless!"

This story has several points of interest, each of which could comprise a dissertation of investigation.

The first observation is, if Jesus was in the temple teaching, why were the most rigid religionists outside of the *ekklesia* (gathering of God's people)? Perhaps they felt their level of knowledge was sufficient. How tragic it is, when those who have a responsibility to lead deduce that what they know is all they need to know.

One philosopher has said, "What you know may be all you know, but it is not all that there is to know."

Secondly, it is strange that these men knew exactly where to find this woman. The text reads that she was "taken in the very act." (KJV) Some things in life are carried out with reckless abandon and flagrant disregard, but adultery is not one of them. The very nature of the interaction dictates surreptitious and clandestine encounters. Was their information the result of an anonymous tip or selective recall?

Thirdly, probably the most trying and disturbing feature of this account is found in the number of persons accused. If indeed the woman was "taken in the very act," where was her partner? Were the prejudices against women so severe that an infraction clearly involving co-conspirators could cause religious leaders to execute one and exonerate the other?

Finally, it is distressing to note the composition of the crowd. It consisted of the aged as well as the young. How unfortunate it is for young people to have few worthy senior examples to imitate, emulate or duplicate. The biblical admonition to "train a child in the way he should go" (Prov. 22:6) suffers brutally at the hands of cold and callous Christians who "stone" sinners in the name of the Lord.

Jesus Dispensed Mercy

The scene then shifted from the angry and bloodthirsty mob, to Jesus who calmly knelt on the ground and began writing in the sand with His finger. The exact content of His transcription has been the source of speculation spanning the years. Pulpits and pulpiteers have risen to heights of unprecedented *isegesis* (imposing an interpretation on the text), or sanctified imagination, in an attempt to decipher what He wrote.

The writer of the story is silent at that point, leaving the content of writing cloudy, but the content of His character unmistakably clear: Sinners can be forgiven. One wonders by the actions of Jesus if He does not raise the rhetorical, "Where is the greater sin?" Which is the most egregious breach of ethics, the adulterer or the executioner?

Bishop S. Chuka Ekeman suggests, "A person is heading for destruction when they see themselves as an island of virtue amidst a sea of unrighteousness.[3]

The crowd demanded justice, but Jesus dispensed mercy.

Justice is "the constant and perpetual disposition of a legal matter,"[4] the impartial levying of remedy in a given situation based on the facts presented, and a concept of fundamental fairness.

Justice will dictate that the driver who inadvertently drove five miles over the posted speed limit would simply hold out his hand and ask for a citation when stopped by an observant and legalistic traffic officer.

Mercy on the other hand has been defined as "unmerited favor." It is an appeal to look beyond facts and fairness and forgo the justifiable consequence for an activity.

The aforementioned driver when stopped by the officer responds with a plea, "I am sorry, I just wasn't paying attention. I really cannot afford to have an infraction on my record. My insurance is already too high!"

A request for mercy appeals to the dispenser of the sentence for a stay of execution.

Jesus was never moved by the pathos of popular opinion. The kingdom of God operates under a theocratic not a democratic model. Operating in the *sub spacia teletocates* (under the gauge of God), Jesus was able to synthesize justice and mercy at every instance and maintain "fidelity to truth and immunity to pressure."[5]

It is here that Jesus begins the process of reconciliation. Although reconciliation is peculiar to the language of the Apostle Paul, he is adept in his analysis of the Master's motives. In 2 Corinthians 5:19, one reads, **God was in Christ reconciling the world to Himself**.

The Greek word *katallasein* (to reconcile) literally means "to change" or "to exchange." It is noteworthy that Paul intensifies the meaning of the word in Ephesians and Colossians by adding the prefix "apo" (*apokallassein*), "to exchange completely." Reconciliation therefore means a complete change in [a person's] relationship to God.[6]

Whereas the woman of the narrative had been excluded from the community of faith, she was included in the communion of the forgiven. This interaction becomes the pragmatic formula for Christ's encounter with fallen humankind.

P.T. Forsyth emphatically asserts:

> Christ came not to say something, but to do something. His revelation was action more than instruction. He revealed by redeeming. The thing He did was not simply to make us aware of God's disposition in an impressive way. It was not to *declare* forgiveness. It was certainly not to *explain* forgiveness. And it was not even to *bestow* forgiveness. It was to *effect* forgiveness and to set up the relation of forgiveness both in God and in Man.[7]

It is here that Christ bestows a threefold blessing upon a broken and bruised beloved of God. His abbreviated conversation with this woman provides an exaggerated measure of grace. Pardon, peace, and prescription are soon to be hers.

Jesus began the conversation by asking, "Where are your accusers?"

And the woman replied, "There are none."

Her response represents pardon for her past. The pardon, or release, from the penalty of past offense is a necessary corrective for the breach that is brought on by sin. It also provides mediation, propitiation, and expiation for the transgressor.

Jesus Was and Is Our Mediator

The pardon of Jesus is obtained through His mediation. The word mediation is defined "to be in the middle."[8] This mediation is twofold. It stands between the accusation and the accused, and it serves before the bar of justice as an advocate over and against the adversary. (1 John 1.)

The second dimension of this pardon is found in its *propitiation*. This word in the New Testament sense is "a covering."[9] (1 John 1.) This covering is not a cover up. The intent of the Gospel is to convey to the penitent believer that the scarlet letter they were consigned to wear has been removed and the spaces covered with the grace of God.

Expiation secures atonement (at-one-ment). This divine pardon puts us again "at one" with God. Estrangement is eliminated, relationship restored, the malady mended.

There is a story told of a little boy who was exceedingly mischievous and on his way to becoming a juvenile delinquent. His father, in an attempt to dramatize the extent of his son's waywardness, stripped a three-foot limb of its bark and branches. They agreed that for every misdeed the father would place a nail in the log.

In ten days the limb was full of nails. When confronted with the incontrovertible evidence the son burst into tears. His father, hoping to redeem him, proposed to his son that for every good deed performed he would remove a nail. In two weeks all the nails were gone. When shown the nail-free limb, the symbol of his reformation, the son began to cry again.

His father was confused and said, "But, son, the nails are gone!"

The boy replied, "Yes, but the holes are still there!"

The father, sensing that he must seize the moment or lose his son to what John Bunyan in Pilgrim's Progress called the "Slough of Despond," interrupted, "Son, these holes say to you that you have not been what you should have been, yet they confirm to me that you're not what you used to be!"[10]

———————————

Singer-songwriter Dottie Rambo, in one of her contemporary hymns, has expressed the joy of pardon appropriated in the following lyrics:

"Amazing Grace" shall always be my song of praise, for it was grace that brought my liberty;

I do not know just why He came to love me so,

He looked beyond my faults and saw my needs."

The Lord moves the encounter to yet a higher plane. His assurance rendered in, **Neither do I condemn thee**, attains peace for her present. Many persons who receive pardon are never able to shake the stigma of an accusing society. One need only to scan the pages of recent history and peruse the post-Watergate life of President Richard Milhouse Nixon. Although the recipient of a presidential pardon, the condemnation of a jaundiced society dogged his steps and hovered over every interview.

Robert Burdette wrote:

> It isn't the experience of today that drives men mad. It is the remorse for something that happened yesterday, and the dread of what tomorrow may disclose.[11]

The absence of peace manifests itself in a number of self-depreciating ways: guilt, worry, frustration, anxiety, humiliation, isolation, estrangement and the like. Without peace, the present is immobilized by a preoccupation with past imperfections.

Shakespeare's Macbeth acted out this scenario with an incessant washing of the hands. Such obsessive compulsive responses are often detected in the repetitive acts of penance found in a restless soul.

The psalmist acknowledged this condition in the confession recorded in Psalm 51:3, **My sin is ever before me**.

William A. Jones in a classic sermon, "The Problem of the Present Past" details the dilemma like this:

> "My sin is ever before me." It's not behind me, it's not even beside me; "My sin is before me" — ever before me, always before me; there's no time that it's not before me. I can't elude it; can't escape it; can't shake it off; can't dismiss it; can't shrug it off. It is glued to my very being. It's on my mind; it's in my heart. My sin is ever before me. It is more than a

matter of memory. I don't call it to remem-
brance. It doesn't have to be called. It's always
present. My past is forever present. *Yesterday
is today.* The *former* is current. *Then is
now!*[12]

The psalmist's personal cosmos was in chaos. The
paralyzing effect of his piercing pronouncement
rendered him dysfunctional and depressed. Peace was
needed in the present. A soothing balm for a bruised
soul was desperately sought in word or deed.

Pardon Brings a Threefold Peace

The noncondemnatory tone of our Lord towards
this woman gave her access to the promise of Jesus in
John 14:27: **Peace I leave with you, my peace I give
you. . . .** Hers was a threefold peace. The "peace of
God" speaks to the internal response to the storms of
the soul.

Philippians 4:7 says that the peace of God
transcends all understanding (NIV). Such peace does
not resort to the stoic posture of the "knight of infinite
resignation," who becomes oblivious to stressors of
the soul, but finds shelter in the time of storm.

> The soul that on Jesus hath leaned for repose,
>   I will not, I will not desert to His foes;
> That soul, though all hell should endeavor to shake,
>   I'll never, no never, no never, forsake.[13]

If the peace of God is an internal manifestation,
then the "peace from God" is an *external* disposition
of grace. Undoubtedly there are times when even the
strongest of internal constitutions needs a cessation
of the external storms of life.

In our focus narrative, the dispersing of the crowd is symbolic of how the Lord can speak to our environments and say, "Peace be still." The winds and the waves are still subject to His will. Turmoil in the homes, frustration on the job, ridicule from your relatives, criticism from the crowd, and the dwindling of resources each can require a supernatural intervention. Perhaps Paul and Timothy's salutation of Philippians 1:2, **Grace be unto you, and peace, from God our Father, and from the Lord Jesus Christ**, was an effort to invoke the zephyr breezes of God's good pleasure upon a faithful people.

The peace trilogy concludes with "peace with God," the external peace. Again the psalmist declared:

Yea, though I walk through the valley of the shadow of death, I will fear no evil for thou art with me.

Psalm 23:4

After surveying the landscape of a mine-field past, great confidence is garnered from the "witness" of God.

There's not an hour that He is not near us
No not one! No not one!
No night so dark but His love can cheer us
No not one! No not one![14]

Finally Jesus provides a prescription for the pilgrimage, "Go and sin no more." This admonition has been the source of much concern and debate among theologians. Rheinhold Niebuhr raises profound inquiry:

The question is whether the grace of Christ is primarily a power of righteousness

99

which so heals the sinful heart that henceforth it is able to fulfill the law of love; or whether it is primarily the assurance of divine mercy for a persistent sinfulness which man never overcomes completely.[15]

Here we believe Jesus pointed to the potential of regenerate believers to set their affections on things above, thus healing the sinful hearts. Yet within the heart rests the inherent possibility of missing the mark. Indeed the Christian is an "absolute paradox."

Within the sinful heart there is placed a desire to be sinless, an earthly creature experiences a heavenly pull, and this animated dust maintains a spark of divinity. Perfection desired, yet mercy is needed. The woman of the text, like us, arises from the dread of despair and struggle, secure on the path of righteousness for His Name's sake. And it is there that we shed the stigma of our sin for a season of grace.

Charles Wesley, in one of his marvelous Elizabethan-language hymns, sought to clarify this:

> Jesus, the First and Last,
> On thee my soul is cast:
> Thou didst Thy work begin
> By blotting out my sin;
>
> Thou wilt the root remove
> And perfect me in love.
>
> Yet when the work is done,
> The work is but begin:
> Partaker of Thy grace,
> I long to see Thy face;
> The first I prove below,
> The last I die to know.

The admonition to "go and sin no more," is a spoken prescription which requires being filled. However, no mere medicinal remedies, apothecarial appropriations, nor pharmaceutical products are sufficient to supply this prescription. Repaired Christians are often placed under surveillance. The key to silencing skeptics and causing cessation to cynical conversation is becoming "owner occupied."

Endnotes

[1] Tenney, *The Expositors Bible Commentary*, Vol. 9

[2] Dodd, Barrett. *Historical Tradition in the Fourth Gospel*, 1953, p. 334.

[3] Sermon.

[4] *Black's Law Dictionary*, (St. Paul, MN: West Publishing Co., 1979), p. 1776.

[5] Brown, M. Pinkney. Introductory remarks at Pennsylvania Avenue A.M.E. Zion Church.

[6] Purkiser, E.T.; Taylor, Richard; and Taylor, Willard H. *God, Man, and Salvation*, (Kansas City: Beacon Hall Press, 1977), pp. 403,404.

[7] Forsyth, P. T., *God the Holy Father*, (London: Independent Press, 1957), p. 19.

[8] *Webster's New Dictionary and Roget's Thesaurus*, p. 449.

[9] Vine's, p. 906.

[10] Spurgeon, Charles H. *Pictures From Pilgrim's Progress*, (Grand Rapids: Baker Book House, 1982 reprint), p. 23.

[11] Burdette, Robert. *Golden Day*.

[12] Jones, William A. *Responsible Preaching*, (Aaron Press, 1989), p. 28.

[13] *Caldwell's Union Harmony*, "How Firm a Foundation," 1837.

[14] Oatman, Johnson. *Prescription for the Beginner*, "There's Not a Friend."

[15] Baillie, John. *Invitation to Pilgrimage*.

8
Owner Occupied

When a dwelling is completed the most imperiling condition in which the new construction can find itself is that of being vacant. Urban blight and rural desolation confirm the hazards of empty houses. Kleptomaniacs incite plunder, pyromaniacs ignite fires and nymphomaniacs excite passions in empty houses.

Analogous to a building without an inhabitant is a newly constructed Christian without the habitation of the Holy Spirit. A most intriguing footnote of Jesus addresses this malady in Luke 11:24-26:

> **When the unclean spirit is gone out of a man, he walketh through dry places, seeking rest; and finding none, he saith, I will return unto my house from whence I came out.**
>
> **And when he cometh, he findeth it swept and garnished.**
>
> **Then goeth he, and taketh to him seven other spirits more wicked than himself; and they enter in, and dwell there; and the last state of that man is worse than the first.**

It is not our intention here to give full treatment to the doctrine of angels or angelology in general, or demons in particular. It is possible to afford integrity to the scriptures without abandoning the advancements that science, technology, psychology, anthropology, and archeology have contributed to our understanding of the biblical world.

Emery H. Bancroft treats the subject of demons assertively in his *Christian Theology*:

> It is evident that the relation of the Scriptures to the doctrine of demons is vital and positive . . . . These teachings are not occasional and incidental, but underlie all biblical history and doctrine. The Bible recognizes not only the material world, but a spiritual world intimately connected with it, and spiritual beings both good and bad who have access to, and influence for good and ill, the world's inhabitants. The testimony of Scripture and what is to be derived from sources outside the Scriptures are mutually confirmatory on this subject. The importance of a careful and unprejudiced consideration of what the Bible teaches is apparent.[1]

In considering the question of manifestation of evil in the earth realm, Dietrich Bonhoeffer, commenting on Genesis 3:1, argued:

> It is not simply said that the serpent is the devil. The serpent is a creature of God, but is more subtle than all the others. In the entire story the devil incarnate is never introduced. And yet evil does take place: through man, through the serpent, through the tree.[2]

The modern mind is anxious to apply psychological and physiological labels to provide explanation for ethical and physical infirmities. The serial killer, child molester, drug abuser, thief, slanderer, adulterer, liar, rapist, car jacker, to name a few, can find appropriate categories of classification in most texts of abnormal psychology or behavioral studies. However, there are few in this enlightened age who would consider the possibility of demonic interference. There is an adherence to scientific orthodoxy to the exclusion of scriptural authority.

The question must be raised:

Why did Jesus speak of and to demons, the devil, and evil?

Was He condescending to the thinking of the age?

Was He intentionally misleading His *followers* for purposes all His own? We think not.

Was He speaking of mere myths? Even if so, one would not need to employ the Bultmannian construct of "demythologizing" the text.

Dr. Andrew Park in a fascinating article entitled "Theo-Orthopraxis" suggests:

> We need to redefine the term myth, and re-enrich theology with myth. Myths point to the reality of the world, even though they do not signify the actuality of the world. While fairy tales are born out of illusion and speculation, myths are born out of actual life-experience, life conflict, and ultimate human questions.[3]

Noted author and psychiatrist M. Scott Peck, dealing with the issue of incarnate evil in his seminal work *People of the Lie*, states:

> In common with 99 percent of psychiatrists and the majority of clergy, I did not

think the devil existed. Still, priding myself on being an open-minded scientist, I felt I had to examine the evidence that might challenge my inclination in the matter. It occurred to me that if I could see one good, old-fashioned case of possession, I might change my mind . . . I now know Satan is real. I met it.[4]

The story of the text, whether it was a manifestation of demonic or evil obsession (influence) or possession (dominance), is a worthwhile investigation for the Christian whose new-found faith may be accurate but not adequate.

Four Compartments of an "Empty House"

The scene in Luke 11:24-26 divides itself into three sequential compartments — the cause, the condition and the consequence. We shall supply the fourth and essential element: the cure. It is at this stage that the Christian is *Owner Occupied*.

1. The unclean spirit went out of the man.

What distinguishes this narrative from all other accounts of demonic confrontations in the Gospels is the voluntary departure of evil. Although the absence was voluntary, it was temporary. Unless sin, evil, and the demonic are exorcised from our senses and cast out of our sensibilities, then its eminent return is assured.

The temptation of Jesus in the wilderness recorded in Luke 4:13 states: . . . **and when the devil had ended all this tempting, he left Him until an opportune time** (NIV).

An opportune time to tempt the Lord of Hosts? Unthinkable! Yet such temptation was unavoidable that the scripture might be fulfilled:

> **. . . Since we have a great high priest who has gone through the heavens, Jesus the Son of God, let us hold firmly to the faith we profess.**
>
> **For we do have a high priest who is able to sympathize with our weaknesses, but we have one who has been tempted in every way, just as we are — yet was without sin.**
>
> **Hebrews 4:14,15 (NIV)**

The coming and going of an evil spirit — conversation, disposition, temper, or lifestyle — is not an experience foreign to most people. The phraseology of "getting up on the right side of the bed" or gaining a "new lease on life" can be manifestations of the fact that your personal demon has decided to leave you alone "until an opportune time."

The text of Luke 11:24-26 suggests that the unclean spirit left the person seeking rest. What was the reason for this demonic exhaustion? Scripture tells us that evil is continually on the prowl to devour the good that God would do in us through the impartation of His Word. Notice Luke 8:5,12 (NIV):

> **A farmer went out to sow his seed. As he was scattering the seed, some fell along the path; it was trampled on, and the birds of the air ate it up . . . .**
>
> **This is the meaning of the parable: The seed is the word of God. Those along the path are the ones who hear, and then the devil comes and takes away the word from their hearts so that they may not believe and be saved.**

Whether the man of the text was a recipient of God's prevenient grace (the drawing), saving grace (the securing), sufficient grace (the sustaining), one thing is certain, he was being exposed to the Word of God. However, before it could take root, it was being snatched up and devoured.

How often have persons been exposed to seminars or sermons that inspire and enervate them to follow "the more excellent way," but as soon as they leave that environment they revert to "business as usual."

The persistence of the man in this text to hear and to have the word of God precipitated the departure of the evil spirit. It needed rest. Within various faith traditions, it is not unusual to hear an exasperated explanation of human depravity with, "The devil is always busy!"

The man's tenacity triumphed. The evil spirit determined there must be easier conquest in the vicinity. He departed, called it quits, went looking for more promising prospects.

Considering this, the words of the Apostle Peter become more relevant:

> **Be sober, be vigilant; because your adversary the devil, as a roaring lion, walketh about, seeking whom he may devour.**
>
> **1 Peter 5:8**

The departure of the unclean spirit left the man without a satanic stain. He now could apply what he was learning without obstruction. His life was taking a turn for the better. He was conforming to the "image of God." Of course this must be understood in context. Bancroft asserts:

> The word *image* does not imply perfect representation in man. Christ is the image of God absolutely. Man is the image of God relatively and derivatively. Since God is Spirit, man made in His image cannot be merely a material thing.[5]

This man had an internal and external transformation. Unfortunately the story does not end at this juncture.

2. The spirit returned after searching dry places.

The plot thickens. The demonic spirit, foiled in his attempt to find another suitable dwelling, returned to the place which he previously called "home." Something has changed, however, for the man (house) is now "swept and garnished."

Swept denotes that he has eliminated unnecessary and cumbersome debris. Indeed "old things" had passed away. He had taken to heart the words of Hebrews 12:1: **. . . Let us lay aside every weight, and the sin which doeth so easily beset us. . . .**

This man was on the road to spiritual success. Donald S. Metz speaks to the issue of spiritual progress:

> The Corinthians had accepted the gospel as a new and revolutionary way of life. Yet many problems persisted in the church. In the Christian life some problems, such as actual sins and transgressions, are solved in the new birth (1 John 3:8-9).
>
> Other problems, such as carnal affections and attitudes, are solved by the cleansing

power of the Holy Spirit in the crisis of entire sanctification. (1 Cor. 3:3; 2 Cor. 7:1; Eph. 5:25-26.) Other problems not related to sin or the carnal mind are solved by spiritual maturity, growth in grace, and enlarged understanding.[6]

3. The "house" (man) was "swept and garnished."

This man was exhibiting growth on every level and was on his way to becoming a paragon of virtue, for not only was he "swept" but "garnished." He now was in possession and display of the decorations of his faith. How often are zealous converts swift to assume the ornamentations and symbols of their faith, while simultaneously lacking the power thereof!

The garnishments of the ancients were as elaborate and noticeable as those of this day, which may include a large Bible under one's arm, a cross around the neck, a sacred charm on the wrist, modest apparel, an exhaustive concordance, and a ready vocabulary of scriptural solutions for life's enigmas.

As striking as this display of emerging "responsible selfhood" was, the unclean spirit was not impressed. Although the man was now unabashedly, unashamedly, and unapologetically a new creation, the demon was not deterred. It made the decision to return to familiar surroundings. However, the demon did not return alone.

4. The spirit brought seven others back with him.

In Luke 11:26, Jesus continued the story of the man who had been delivered from demonic bondage:

> **Then goeth he, and taketh to him seven other spirits more wicked than himself; and they**

**enter in, and dwell there: and the last state of
that man is worse than the first.**

Since the dwelling had been emptied of debris
and rummage, it afforded room for more inhabitants.
Scientists contend that nature abhors a vacuum.
Apparently this is also true in the spiritual realm.

It is alarming to hear of such compound wickedness or schizophrenia of the spirit, yet it was not
unique in those days.

Luke 8:26ff gives an account of a man called
"Legion" because of the multitude of spirits residing
within him. Nor can one forgot Mary Magdalene,
from whom seven unclean spirits were exorcised.
(Luke 8:2.)

There are many of this day who feel besieged and
beset upon by what appear to be a plethora of
malevolent miscreants. For them, one vice or one
infirmity is not enough. The body, soul, and spirit must
simultaneously be engaged in sociopathic, psycho-
pathic, maladaptive, sinful behavior. What a terrible
state in which to find oneself.

The real tragedy, however, is not the current
condition of the man, as dreadful as it is. The tragedy
lies in the fact that he had gotten better, then took a
turn for the worse.

His dreams were dashed,
visions vanished,
enlightenment extinguished
and his witness wrecked.

All too often people submit themselves to the drawing of the Holy Spirit, join a church, improve their inter- and intra-personal relationships only to become "worse" than they were before.

At that point, there are those who would argue that the man would have been better were he left alone. To that position we take exception.

The Ending Can Be Hopeful

Although Jesus ended the parable on a note of despair, it certainly did not *have* to end that way. The tragic flaw of this convert under construction was that the dwelling was complete, yet incomplete. Our intention is not to give a treatise on Pneumatology (the doctrine of the Holy Spirit) but of being "filled with the Spirit."

> To the men who wrote the New Testament, and to those for whom they wrote, the Spirit was not a doctrine but an experience. Their watchword was not, "Believe in the Holy Ghost," but "Receive ye the Holy Ghost." Our attempts to justify the exclusion of the Holy Spirit from our lives may be thoughtful and eloquent, but it leaves one shallow and impotent. To walk in the Spirit realm without the Holy Spirit is as futile as attempting to live in the aquatic realm without external air supply.[7]

George E. Ladd, commenting on the necessity of the Holy Spirit, wrote:

> The contrast between the realm above and that below is the contrast between the realm of the Holy Spirit and the realm of

human existence . . . the same contrast has already appeared in the saying about the new birth: **That which is born of flesh is flesh and that which is born of Spirit is Spirit** (John 3:6). The flesh is not evil, it is simply incapable in itself of reaching up to the world of God and grasping divine realities.[8]

The infilling of the Holy Spirit, although internal and essential, is not devoid of external evidence. Professor James Forbes in his Yale lectures posits:

> When one claims to be anointed with the Holy Spirit, wholeness should be a noticeable feature. Just as the oil was poured on Aaron's head and went down to the skirts of his garment, so the oil of the Spirit covers all that we are and have. As Christians yielding to the Spirit, our total beings are transformed, and no area of life is excluded from the process. Wholehearted dedication and commitment of the collective aspects of our being are in evidence.[9]

One may ask how the Holy Spirit is appropriated into the life of the believer? Jesus gives clear and complete instruction in this matter in Luke 11:9,10:

> **And I say unto you, Ask, and it shall be given you; seek, and ye shall find; knock, and it shall be opened unto you.**
>
> **For every one that asketh receiveth; and he that seeketh findeth; and to him that knocketh it shall be opened.**

Jesus gave the confirmation of the Spirit indwelling to those who would believe in John 14:16,17:

And I will pray the Father, and he shall give you another Comforter, that he may abide with you forever;

Even the Spirit of truth; whom the world cannot receive, because it seeth him not, neither knoweth him: but ye know him; for he dwelleth with you, and shall be in you.

Once the Holy Spirit has been invited to take up residence in the heart of the believer, no power on earth can subdue or sabotage the newly constructed Christian for **. . . greater is He that is in you, than he that is in the world** (1 John 4:4).

You have now become *Owner Occupied*, and can say with A. Reed:

> Holy Ghost with light divine,
> Shine upon this guilty heart of mine;
> Chase the shades of night away,
> Turn my darkness into Day.
>
> Holy Ghost with power divine,
> Cleanse this guilty heart of mine;
> Long hath sin without control,
> Held dominion o'er my soul.
>
> Holy Ghost, with joy divine,
> Cheer this saddened heart of mine;
> Bid my many woes depart,
> Heal my wounded, bleeding heart.
>
> Holy Spirit all divine,
> Dwell within this heart of mine;
> Cast down every idol throne,
> Reign supreme and Reign Alone.[10]

Endnotes

[1] Bancroft, Emery H. *Christian Theology*, (Grand Rapids: Zondervan Publishing House), pp. 313,314.

[2] Bonhoeffer, Dietrich. *Creation and Fall Temptation*, (New York: MacMillan Publishing Co., 1959), p. 66.

[3] Park, Andrew Sung. *Journal of Theology*, "Theo-Ortho Pratis," United Theological Seminary, 1993.

[4] Peck, M. Scott. *People of the Lie*, (New York: Simon and Schuster, 1983), pp. 182,183.

[5] Bancroft, p. 191.

[6] *God, Man, and Salvation*, p. 511.

[7] Harrison, Everett F., Ed. in Chief. *Baker's Dictionary of Theology*, (Grand Rapids: Baker Book House, 1960), p. 494.

[8] Ladd, George Eldon. *A Theology of the New Testament*, (New York: William B. Eerdmans Publishing Co., 1974), p. 42.

[9] Forbes, James. *The Holy Spirit and Preaching*, (Nashville: Abingdon Press, 1989), pp. 47,48.

[10] Reed, A.

9
The Master Builder

We live in a culture which seems to suggest the highest virtue is autonomy. Walker Percy may yet be imminently correct in declaring we live in what may be called "the century of the self."[1] In Western culture, we are taught to be self-reliant, self-made. Our goal in working hard, whether for wages or weight reduction, is to be self-actualized, self-fulfilled.

Any desire or need for assistance is considered a sign of weakness. When a person can proclaim, "I am doing just fine by myself," this is understood as an indication of emotional health and maturity.

Thus far in our attempt to raise some salient suggestions for spiritual growth and maturation, we have emphasized subjective volitional acts. We have discussed the necessity of cost counting, laying a solid foundation, compliance with spiritual specifications, and so forth. These are all essential, but not sufficient.

The fact of the matter is we can do very little on our own. Even if we have good intentions and plan with purpose, our efforts may be scuttled. In reality, we are what Friedreich Schleiermacher described as "absolutely dependent upon the Absolute and ultimately dependent upon the Ultimate."[2]

Foundationally, our very beings rest upon God.[3] When all is said and done, we must confess "all that we are or ever hope to be – to God be the glory for the things He has done."

Yet, there is a constant temptation to resort to human ingenuity. The attraction is to take matters into our own hands, only to rediscover that we are mere frail, feeble creatures of dust, unable to make it alone. Thus, we see there are things for which we must look to God.

Returning from a visit to a rural village in central Malawi, a group of short-term missionaries found themselves being held hostage to the forces of nature.

They could not pass along the road because a rushing stream from Mount Soche had washed out the road. There they sat in modern vehicles, helpless humanity unable to traverse the tide, totally dependent on a merciful God to cause a recession of the mighty flowing water.

We are reminded by the psalmist in the 127th Psalm of the fallacy of excluding God from the construction process.

> **Except the Lord build the house, they labour in vain that build it: except the Lord keep the city, the watchman waketh but in vain.**
>
> **It is vain for you to rise up early, to sit up late, to eat the bread of sorrows: for so he giveth his beloved sleep.**
>
> **Lo, children are an heritage of the Lord: and the fruit of the womb is his reward.**
>
> **As arrows are in the hand of a mighty man; so are children of the youth.**

Happy is the man that hath his quiver full of them: they shall not be ashamed, but they shall speak with the enemies in the gate.

Psalm 127:1-5

Even in Christian service, we can start projects of our own: erecting crystal cathedrals, launching growth campaigns, paying significant amounts of money, visiting homeless shelters. However, if these projects are not of God, they are for naught.

It has been said "Little is much if God is in it," but the converse is also true, "Much is nothing, if God is not in it."[4] This is the point we are attempting to make.

Psalm 127 emphatically says that, unless our activity is directed by God, it is a waste of time and energy. "Man proposes but God disposes." A disproportionate amount of what we engage in is "much ado about nothing."

Four Spiritual Dimensions of Christian Construction

Four common activities of life are chosen by the psalmist to illustrate his point. They are *house construction, civil defense, general employment, and family development*.

Construction of the spiritual dimension in each individual is analogous to these activities.

A house can be built in two ways:

1. Once plans based on one's own knowledge, skill, and financial resources are implemented, and the structure is completed, then ask God's blessings.

2. An alternative is to wait until the Lord has given unmistakable instruction, then proceed with conscious dependence on Him.

In the first instance, the project never goes beyond flesh and blood.

In the second, there is the thrill of seeing God working through the marvelous provision of needed supplies, through the miraculous timing and sequence of events, and through the converging circumstances that would never happen according to the laws of chance.[5]

Building with God makes all the difference in the world. This is equally true, if not more so, of the soul.

He who walks and works with God, will never walk or work alone. There is no spiritual construction which can be successful without the Master Builder.

Human effort is futile without God in the area of security. There is no protective agency or societal instrumentality which can prevent harm. Ultimately, our safety lies in the Lord, and unless we are really depending on Him, our ordinary precautions are not enough to provide security.

As in the days of Nehemiah (Neh. 4-6), there are those who were adversarial to the construction process. Even in the midst of the erection of walls for faith, fortification forces will arise against you. These forces come on two fronts. Often there is opposition from without and abuse from within.

When word goes out that Christian construction is in progress there is a tendency for others to become furious and very indignant. They may even mock and ridicule the effort. All sorts of questions regarding your labor may be raised.

What is she doing?

Is she trying to act like a Christian?

Who does she think she is anyway?

Just remember, "If God be for you, who can be against you?"

When ridicule, rumor, and recrimination fail to daunt the process, persons may resort to threat of attack. Conspiratorial plots and schemes to create confusion can occur. Nevertheless make your prayer to God.

Also, be careful of opposition through discouragement. This ploy is one of the adversary's chief weapons. He uses it most often and against everyone without regard to race, gender, or age. Do not be afraid, but remember the Lord is great and awesome. If necessary engage in the solution of self-talk. Say to your soul, in the words of the well-known song:

"The Storm Is Passing Over"

Take courage, my soul, and let us journey on.
Though the night is dark, it won't be very long.
Thanks be to God, the morning light appears.
And the storm is passing over, hallelujah!

In our chosen occupations and everyday employment, it is futile to labor long hours, earning one's living through anxious toil, unless we are in the place of God's choosing. Please do not misunderstand.

Scripture teaches us to diligently work to supply our needs, those of our family and others. We are not advocating sloth. Neither are we suggesting or encouraging a life of leisure sponging off friends and relations.

The point is simple: Working independent of God, we do not and cannot really advance. An apt biblical description of the situation can be found in Haggai 1:6:

> **Ye have sown much, and bring in little; ye eat, but ye have not enough; ye drink, but ye are not filled with drink; ye clothe you, but there is none warm; and he that earneth wages earneth wages to put it into a bag with holes.**

However, if we really yield to the Lord and live for His glory, He is able to bestow gifts while we are sleeping which would not be possible through long, weary hours of labor without Him. This is antithetical to the notion:

> The height of great people reached and kept is done by sudden flight. But they, while their companions slept, were toiling upward in the night.[7]

Remember: **For so he giveth his beloved sleep** (Ps. 127:2b).

As it relates to domestic stability and home life, no amount of legislative posturing or other discussion will be able to restore family values. Much of what is ailing the contemporary household and contributing to decadence in the home is due to our benign (and sometimes, in society, malign) exclusion of God. An exclusion made "rational" through empty rhetoric and superfluous philosophically spun "reasons."

We attempt to compensate for God's absence in the home in various and sundry ways. We shower our children with gadgets for entertainment for temporary appeasement. Introducing our children to God through family prayer, church school or worship never crosses the minds of many parents today. These all seem antiquated relics of pre-modernity. However, those are the things needed most.

The fourth and final illustration the psalmist gives is regarding the *building of a family*. Herein lies the solution to our present-day family crisis.

Lo, children are an heritage of the Lord; and the fruit of the womb is his reward.

Psalm 127:3

This saying about children presupposes they have been reared in a God-fearing home where the Lord is granted deference and obeyed. Children should be brought up in the discipline and instruction of the Lord. Failure to do so could result in enormous heartache rather than a blessing.

We may well attempt to construct though the usual means of eradication of surface debris, excavation of subsurface hindrance, elevation of walls, and extenuation of a roof but these do not in themselves complete a building. Zechariah reiterated:

Not by might, nor by power, but by My Spirit, saith the Lord of hosts.

Zechariah 4:6

There is a tendency to rely on the perceived power of money or on human ingenuity, neither of which can bring the Lord's will to fruition. We can only build for eternity by His spirit. It is not what we do for God through our own resources, all we have comes from Him, but what He does through us is by His mighty power.

The best we can produce is brick, wood, hay, stubble. In the Master's hand we can become producers of gold, silver, and precious gems. (1 Cor. 3:11-15.) When we act autonomously in our own strength, we are going in circles. Our lives become exceptionally efficient when we bring God into everything.

Carnal consequences are yielded by carnal tools.

Spiritual results are spawned by spiritual instruments.

Except the lord build the house, they labour in vain who build it (Ps. 127:1a).

All our strivings may be after wind for "the blessings of the Lord enriches, and toil adds nothing to it."[8] The only plausible conclusion to the matter of constructing Christian character is relinquishing responsibility for the process to God.

We as humans are ill-equipped to be certified as contractors or builders of pristine personality and sterling soul. Such worthy work can not be trusted to mere mortals. Only the Master of mortality and the Initiator of immorality can accomplish such a phenomenal feat.

Endnotes

[1]Percy, Walker, author, lecturer, and professor at Emory University, Atlanta.

[2]Schleiermacher, Friedreich. *The Christian Faith*, (Edinburgh: T. PT. Clark, 1928).

[3]Tillich, Paul. *The Shaking of the Foundations*, (New York: Charles Scribner Sons, 1956.)

[4]MacDonald, William. *Believer's Bible Commentary*, (Nashville: Thomas Nelson Pub., Inc., 1940), p. 755.

[5]Ibid, p. 756.

[6]Tindley, Charles. "Covenant My Soul."

[7]Longfellow, H.W. "The Ladder of St. Augustine."

[8]McCann, Clint Jr. *A Logical Introduction to the Book of Psalms*, (Nashville: Abingdon Press, 1993), p. 40.